DEDICATION

This book is dedicated to my companion, friend, and wife with whom I have shared the pleasures of the last 20 years.

An unusual condition exists throughout Hawaii regarding highway numbers. Pick up five highway maps of the islands and the chances are good that they will not show the same highway numbers. In this book, on the maps and in the driving instructions for each hike, I have used the route numbers posted on the highway. In some instances, I have made note of this problem in the driving instructions. There are not many roads on any of the islands except Oahu, so you are not likely to be confused or to get lost if you use good judgment.

Wailua Falls

HIKING KAUAI

The Garden Isle

by Robert Smith

 Wilderness Press
BERKELEY

First edition 1977
Second edition 1979
THIRD EDITION 1983
Fourth printing March 1987

Copyright © 1977, 1979, 1983 by Robert Smith
Maps by Kevin G. Chard
Front-cover photo and drawings by Patrick Duffy
Design by Thomas Winnett
Library of Congress Card Catalog Number 83-60684
International Standard Book Number 0-89997-031-1
Manufactured in the United States
Published by Wilderness Press
           2440 Bancroft Way
           Berkeley CA 94704
Photo Credits:
Robert Smith 5, 20, 23, 42, 49, 61, 67, 73, 81, 97, 100
Hawaiian Visitors Bureau ii, 2, 14, 31, 35, 38, 51, 53, 91
Ron Felzer 18, 19, 64, 74, 87, 93
Patrick Duffy viii, 28, 56, 95
Ralph Daehler 21, 88

ACKNOWLEDGEMENTS

I am indebted to a number of people who generously offered their time and effort to make this book possible, Ralph E. Daehler, District Forester for the State of Hawaii, contributed his knowledge and the resources of his department. I am particularly grateful for his patience and good humor in response to my queries and requests. A very special *mahalo* to Roy Fujioka for sharing his knowledge of the island and, along with Carol his wife, for their generosity. Many thanks to Nancy, my wife, for typing the manuscript and to Lou Mellencamp for his professional advice and assistance on the photos in this book.

—*Robert Smith*
Huntington Beach, CA
February, 1977

Other books by Robert Smith
from Wilderness Press

Hiking Hawaii: The Big Island
Hiking Maui: The Valley Isle
Hiking Oahu: The Capital Isle
Hawaii's Best Hiking Trails

Contents

Part I: Introduction
  The Island   1
  Using This Book   3
  Hiking Chart   6
  Camping   7
  Food and Equipment   11

Part II: Hiking Trails on Kauai
  1. Kalalau Trail   17
  2. Lumahai Beach   34
  3. Hanalei River   36
  4. Moloaa Beach   39
  5. Keahua Trails   41
  6. Nonou Mountain   52
  7. Lydgate Park   57
  8. Wailua Falls   60
  9. Kilohana Crater   63
  10. Poipu Beach Petroglyphs   66
  11. Kukuiolono Park   68
  12. Waimea   70
  13. Polihale State Park   72
  14. Kokee State Park/Waimea Canyon   75
          (Berry Flat Trail, Puu Ka Ohelo Trail, Black
          Pipe Trail, Canyon Trail, Cliff Trail, Ditch
          Trail, Halemanu-Kokee Trail, Iliau Nature
          Loop, Kaluahaulu-Waialae Trail, Kaluapuhi
          Trail, Koaie Canyon Trail, Kukui Trail,
          Kumuwela Trail, Waialae Canyon Trail,
          Waimea Canyon Trail, Wainininua Trail,
          Alakai Swamp, Awaawapuhi Trail, Honopu
          Trail, Kawaikoi Stream Trail, Maile Flat
          Trail, Mohihi-Waialae Trail, Nualolo Trail,
          Pihia Trail, Poomau Canyon, Waialeale Wil-
          derness Trail)

Appendix   104
Index   105

Part I: Introduction

Kauai

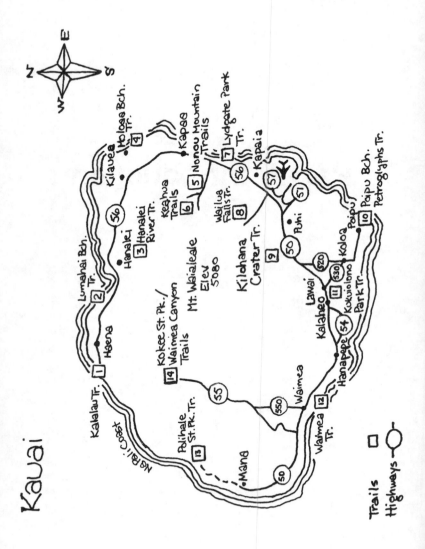

Trails □
Highways ⬭○

The Island

Some people call it Kauai-a-mamo-ka-lani-pō—"The fountainhead of many waters from on high and bubbling up from below." Others regard it as "The Grand Canyon of the Pacific" or "The Garden Island" and still others say it is "The land of the Menehune." But even if you just call it "Kauai"—time of plenty, or fruitful season—it is still a land of beauty, grandeur and adventure, and a challenge to the outdoorsman. There is a lot of hiking pleasure packed in to this almost circular little island of 555 square miles.

Kauai lays claim to a number of firsts and unique characteristics. It is the oldest island in the Hawaiian Islands, it is the northern-most inhabited island in the chain, and it was the first one visited by Captain Cook—though that is a rather dubious distinction. Still other things of local pride include Mt. Waialeale, the wettest spot on earth; the only place on earth where the iliau, a rare and unique plant, is to be found; and the home of the legendary Menehune, a race of pygmies who were short, industrious, strong, and highly skilled workers in stone.

Not unlike the neighboring islands, tourism on Kauai with its 39,000 inhabitants has grown to the point that over 800,000 people annually visit it. Kauai lies 102 air miles northwest of Honolulu—about a 20-minute flight. Most visitors to Kauai are seeking its solitude and slower pace of life, and many find these in the verdant valleys of the remote Na Pali coast and in the lush canyon lands of Waimea. Conveniently, the State of Hawaii and the County of Kauai have established miles of trails and jeep roads into remote areas which will reveal some of the island's secrets.

Spouting horn, a natural sea geyser

Using This Book

With few exceptions, hiking on Kauai does not require any special equipment or skill. Many places are readily accessible even to the tenderfoot and to people not inclined to hike much. The hikes included in this guide are in four categories, and a glance at the Hiking Chart below will enable you to make a decision based on your interests, your skill, and the time you wish to devote to your hike. The "Family Hikes" are short, easy strolls for people with small children and people who are unaccustomed to strenuous activity. Hikes in the "Hardy Family" category require some effort, and sound physical condition. Hikes in the "Strenuous" and the "Difficult" classifications are more serious hikes, and require not only sound physical condition but also good footwear and sometimes additional equipment. Most of them are full-day or overnight hikes.

The Hiking Chart provides the information necessary for a person to choose a hike. It includes one-way trail time and distance, elevation gain, if any, and equipment needed. Obviously, trail time depends on your pace and physical condition, and the time you devote to sightseeing or swimming. The time given is based on a leisurely pace, including time to picnic, to swim and to explore.

The trail rating in the Hiking Chart is based on whether there is a trail that is either maintained or sufficiently traveled so that it is distinguishable. However, do not be discouraged by a "rough" or "no trail" rating, for in many cases a stream or some readily identifiable physical characteristic marks the way.

Driving time and mileage are based on the posted speed limit and are measured from Lihue, the center of tourist activity and the county seat. (Kauai is a county.) Specific driving instructions for each hike appear with that hike. There is no public transportation on the island. At present, hitchhiking is allowed, although the county council raises the issue from time to time, and may prohibit it in the future. Check with the Hawaiian Visitors Bureau information booth at the airport regarding the law. If you hitchhike, be patient, for rides are hard to come by in the outlying areas.

For most hikes your only needs are food, water, a first-aid kit, and sound footwear. Although hiking boots are not essential on most hikes, I wear them because I am particularly fond of my feet, and I recommend them. Water is available from streams in many areas, but should be boiled or treated before drinking. Cattle, pigs and goats usually share the stream water with you. I suggest you begin each hike with one quart of water per person. Due to the heavy rainfall on Kauai, dry firewood is rare, so a small, light, reliable backpacking stove is a convenience and a comfort. A hot cup of tea, coffee or soup is invigorating while waiting out a passing storm, and a hot breakfast is desirable after a wet night. Lastly, most hikers find shorts or cutoffs adequate on most trails. However, along the Kalalau Trail most people shed all clothing for either physical or psychological reasons—I have not decided which.

In the text preceding a trial description is a map to help you get to the trailhead. These maps are not exactly to scale but are drawn to emphasize important features. For each hike, I give the hike's features as well as camping information (where applicable), hiking distance and time, driving instructions, special instructions, and introductory notes about the hike.

In the trail description, I usually mention the flora and fauna along the trail, particularly the unusual and the unique, in hopes of adding to your hiking enjoyment. But I mention only a few examples, and you may wish to buy one or several small guides to plants and animals common to the islands. These are available at many stores on the island.

Coral ginger

Hiking Chart

Hiking Area Number		Hike Rating				Trail Time			Trail Rating			From Lihue		Equipment					Features				
		Family	Hardy family	Strenuous	Difficult	Distance (miles)	Time (hours)	Gain (feet)	Good trail	Rough trail	No trail	Miles	Time (hours)	Ranger	Boots recommended	Tennis Shoes O.K.	Carry Water	Take Food	Swimming	Waterfalls	Views	Historical Sites	Fruits
1	Kalalau Trail											38	1										
	to Hanakapiai		X			2	1		X						X	X	X	X	X		X		X
	Hanakapiai Loop Tr.		X			1.3	1		X							X	X		X			X	X
	to Hanakapiai Falls				X	1.3	1½			X					X	X	X		X	X	X			X
	to Hanakoa				X	4	2½		X					X	X		X	X	X	X	X	X	X
	to Hanakoa Falls				X	.4	1/4			X						X	X	X	X	X			
	to Kalalau Beach				X	4.8	3		X					X	X		X	X	X	X	X	X	X
2	Lumahai Beach	X				.2	1/6		X			33	3/4					X	X		X		
3	Hanalei River	X				1.3	3/4			X		31	3/4			X	X	X	X		X		X
4	Moloaa Beach	X				1.5	1		X			18	1/2		X	X	X	X	X		X		X
5	Nonou Mountain																						
	Eastside		X			2	1½	1250	X			7	1/4	X	X	X	X	X			X		
	Westside		X			1.5	1	1000	X			10	1/2	X	X	X	X	X			X		
6	Keahua Trails																						
	Keahua Arboretum	X				.5	1/2		X			12	1/2	X			X	X	X				
	Moalepe Tr.		X			2.5	1½	500	X			12	1/2		X	X	X	X			X		X
	Kuilau Ridge Tr.		X			2.1	1½		X			12	1/2		X	X	X	X			X		X
7	Lydgate Park	X				1	1		X			6	1/4					X	X			X	X
8	Wailua Falls				X	.5	1/2				X	5	1/3				X	X	X	X	X	X	X
9	Kilohana Crater		X			2.5	1½	1000	X			4	1/4	X			X	X			X	X	X
10	Poipu Beach Petroglyphs	X				1	1/2				X	14	1/2			X	X	X	X		X	X	
11	Kukuiolono Park	X				.5	1/2				X	12	1/2					X			X	X	
12	Waimea (Russian Fort)	X				.5	1/2		X			22	3/4					X	X		X	X	
13	Polihale State Park		X			3	1½				X	38	1			X	X	X	X		X	X	
14	Kokee/Waimea Canyon											38	1½										
	Southeast																						
	Berry Flat Tr.	X				1	1/2		X						X	X	X	X					
	Black Pipe Tr.		X			.4	1/2			X					X	X	X	X			X		
	Canyon Rr.			X		1.7	2	800	X					X			X	X	X	X	X		
	Cliff Tr.	X				.1	1/6		X							X	X				X		
	Ditch Tr.			X		3.5	4			X				X	X		X	X			X	X	X
	Halemanu-Kokee Tr.	X				1.2	1		X						X	X	X	X					X
	Iliau Nature Loop Tr.	X				.3	1/4		X								X			X	X		
	Kaluahaulu-Waialae Tr.				X	7	FD*			X				X			X	X	X		X	X	
	Kaluapuhi Tr.		X			1.7	1½		X					X	X	X	X						X
	Koaie Canyon Tr.				X	3	2			X				X			X	X	X	X	X	X	X
	Kukui Tr.			X		2.5	2	2000	X					X			X	X	X		X	X	X
	Kumuwela Tr.			X		.8	1	300	X						X	X	X	X					
	Puu Ka Ohelo Tr.	X				.3	1/4		X							X	X	X					X
	Waialae Canyon Tr.			X		.3	1/2			X				X			X	X			X	X	
	Waimea Canyon Tr.			X		1.5	2		X					X			X	X	X		X	X	
	Waininiua Tr.	X				.6	1/2		X						X	X	X	X					
	Northwest																						
	Alakai Swamp Tr.			X		3.4	3			X				X	X		X	X			X		
	Awaawapuhi Tr.			X		3.3	3		X					X	X		X	X			X		
	Honopu Tr.			X		2.5	2½			X				X	X		X	X			X		
	Kawaikoi Stream Tr.	X				1.3	3/4		X					X	X	X			X				X
	Maile Flat Tr.	X				1.3	1		X					X	X	X	X	X			X		
	Mohihi-Waialae Tr.				X	9	FD*			X				X	X		X	X			X		
	Nualolo Tr.			X		4.0	3	1500		X				X	X		X	X			X		
	Pihea Tr.			X		3.3	3		X					X	X		X	X			X		
	Poomau Canyon Tr.	X				.3	1/4		X					X	X	X	X				X	X	
	Mt. Waialeale Tr.				X	6	FD*	1500			X			X	X		X	X			X	X	

*Full-day hike

Camping

Camping out on Kauai will add another dimension to your visit. Campgrounds on Kauai range from adequate to good, contain most of the amenities, and are either free or cheap. The accompanying map locates and cites the facilities available at state and county campgrounds. A third jurisdiction, the Division of Forestry, also provides a number of campgrounds, camping shelters, and camping areas, which are noted on individual maps throughout the book. A word about each kind of campground should be helpful.

First, the Hawaii State Parks at Kokee and Polihale offer excellent facilities and are free. Camping is limited to five days per 30-day period for each campground, and is by permit only, obtained through the Department of Land & Natural Resources, Division of State Parks, Room 306, in the State Building in Lihue (3060 Eiwa St.); or if you choose to write for a permit, write to P.O. Box 1671, Lihue, Kauai 96766. When writing for reservations, include the dates desired, the park, the number of persons and their names. The state cabins at Kokee State Park are operated by a concessionaire (see Hiking Area No. 18 for details). Recently, Kalalau Valley came under the jurisdiction of the state parks. There are no facilities in Kalalau, although wilderness camping is permitted. Permits are limited to five nights per 30-day period, and must be secured through the Division of State Parks (address above).

Secondly, the County of Kauai has numerous campgrounds and beach parks around the island. County camping costs $3 per adult per day. Persons under 18 are free if accompanied by an adult. Permits are not issued to persons under 18. Camping permits are issued for four days, and can be renewed for four more. No person will be issued a permit for more than 12 days during any one year. For reservations, write Department of Parks and Recreation (see Appendix). Include your name, address, campground desired, dates, number of persons in your party, with names and ages, and the $3 fee per adult per day. Camping is free if you have been a Kauai county resident for one year. Although reservations may be made by mail, all permits must be picked up in person at the County Portable Building #5 opposite the convention hall in Lihue or, when closed, at the Kauai Police Department nearby.

Last, the Hawaii State Division of Forestry maintains a number of trailside camping areas in the forest reserve, which are identified on the individual maps preceding the text of each hiking area. Camping is limited to three nights within a 30-day period, but this regulation is not regularly enforced. Neither permits nor reservations are necessary. Registration is by sign-in at the trailhead upon entering and leaving a forest-reserve area. All the facilities are primitive and lacking in amenities, but to some people that is their best feature.

The Division of State Parks regulates camping along the Na Pali Coast: Hanakapiai, Hanakoa, Kalalau—the three major valleys along the wilderness trail. Camping permits are required and may be obtained from the Department of Land & Natural Resources. Camping is limited to five nights total along the Na Pali Coast in any 30-day period. Hanakapiai and Hanakoa are limited to one night each in that period.

My advice is to stay at the state parks—Kokee or Polihale—when possible, for they are conveniently situated, the best campgrounds on the island, and free. Of the county campgrounds, Salt Pond is very good, and Haena and Hanamaulu are satisfactory.

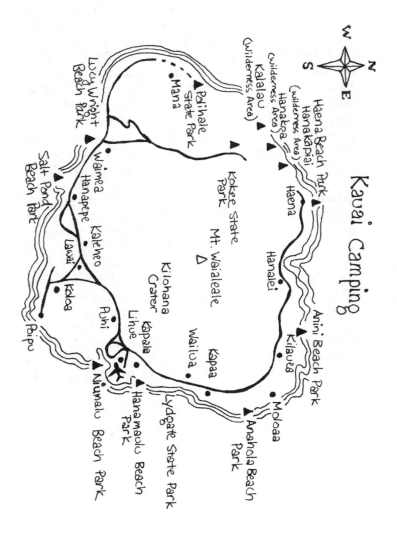

Kauai Camping

Campers are well advised to bring their own equipment because locally it is expensive. There are two equipment rental companies on the island. Bob's Bargain Rentals is located near the airport in Nawiliwili (P.O. Box 3208, Lihue, Hi. 96766, tel. 808/245-9211) and Hanalei Camping & Backpacking is located in Hanalei, Hi. 96714, tel. 808/826-6664). One alternative is to rent a fully equipped camper, which provides both your transportation and camping equipment. For information write Beach Boy Campers, P.O. Box 3208, Lihue, Hi. 96766. Mobile homes and campers are permitted only at Kokee and Polihale state parks, and at Haena, Hanamaulu and Niumalu county parks.

Camping in Hawaii has always been an enjoyable and inexpensive way to experience the Islands. Recently, however, some campers have been beaten and a few have been killed. Most of the beatings have been committed by local men, according to the victims. No one has been convicted of any killings. Most of the assaults have taken place at campgrounds that were close to cities or towns where locals congregate. There has been little or no problem in remote and wilderness areas or in the national parks. The best advice is to avoid camping in areas readily accessible to locals and to avoid contact with groups of people.

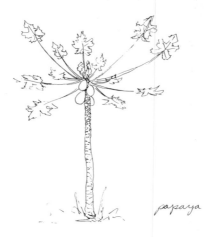

papaya

Food and Equipment

Although food is more expensive on Kauai than on the mainland, it is readily available in most of the towns. You may visit a local delicatessen that repares box lunchs containing local favorites such as tempura, sweet-and-sour spare ribs and sushi—Japanese rice balls containing vegetables and wrapped in seaweed. When fruits are not available along the trail, be certain to visit a local market for mango, papaya, pineapple, passion fruit, and local avocado which comes in the large economy size.

The short-term visitor and the casual hiker do not need a lot of sophisticated hiking equipment. For a day hike, the following equipment is recommended.

Knapsack
Hiking boots or tennis shoes
Canteen, quart size (one per person)
Scout or Swiss Army knife
Insect repellent
Shorts
Bathing suit
Sunburn lotion or preventative
Sun glasses
Whistle for each child
Camera and film
Hiking Kauai—The Garden Isle
Optional: (but oh so nice to have!)
  Poncho or other raingear
  Hat or bandana
  Towel
  Waterproof matches

Although the backpacker or overnight hiker visiting the island may have had previous experience, here are some items of equipment and some tips that should prove helpful.

BACKPACK CHECKLIST

General Equipment:
Frame and pack
Lightweight sleeping bag or blanket
Nylon backpack tent—it rains a lot in most areas
Plastic ground cover—the ground is damp in most areas
Foam pad
Canteen—quart size
Scout or Swiss Army knife
Flashlight
40 feet of nylon cord
First-aid kit

Cooking Gear
Backpack stove
Fuel
Cooking pots
Sierra cup
Waterproof matches

Clothing
Poncho or raingear—A MUST
Pants, shorts or bathing suit
Hat or bandana
Underwear
Socks
Hiking boots

Toilet Articles
Soap (biodegradable)
Toothbrush/powder-paste
Part-roll of toilet paper
Chapstick
Comb
Washcloth and towel
Insect repellent
Sunburn lotion or preventative

Miscellaneous
Sun glasses
Camera and film
Plastic bags
Fishing gear

Hiking is pleasurable when the hiker has taken the time to plan his trip and to prepare his equipment.

Hawaiian Made Easy

For your interest, throughout the text wherever a Hawaiian place name is used, I have provided a literal translation if possible. In many instances, Hawaiian names have multiple meanings and even the experts sometimes disagree over the literal meaning. The meanings given here are based on the best information available and on the context in which the name is used. As students of the environment, the Hawaiians had a flair for finding the most expressive words to describe their physical surroundings.

Most visitors are reluctant to try to pronounce Hawaiian words. But with a little practice and a knowledge of some simple rules, you can develop some language skill and add to your Hawaiian experience. Linguists regard Hawaiian as one of the most fluid and melodious languages of the world. There are only 12 letters in the Hawaiian alphabet: five vowels, a,e,i,o,u, and seven consonants, h,k,l,m,n,p,w. Hawaiian is spelled phonetically. Correct pronunciation is easy if you do not try to force English pronunciation onto the Hawaiian language. Vowel sounds are simple: a=ah; e=eh; i=ee; o=oh; and u=oo. Consonant sounds are the same as in English with the exception of w. Rules for w are not adhered to with any consistency by local people. Generally, w is pronounced "w" at the beginning of a word and after a. For example. Waimea is pronounced "Wai-may-ah" and wala-wala is "Wah-lah-wah-lah." Hawaiians also usually pronounce w as "w" when it follows o or u; auwaha is "ah-oo-wah-hah," and hoowali is "hoh-oh-wah-lee." When w is next to the final letter of a word, it is variably pronounced "w" and "v"; Wahiawa is "wah-he-ah-wa," but Hawi is "ha-vee." Listen to the locals for their treatment of this sound. Since the Hawaiian language is not strongly accented, the visitor will probably be understood without employing any accent.

Kilauea Lighthouse—northernmost point on Hawaiian Islands

Part II:

Hiking Trails on Kauai

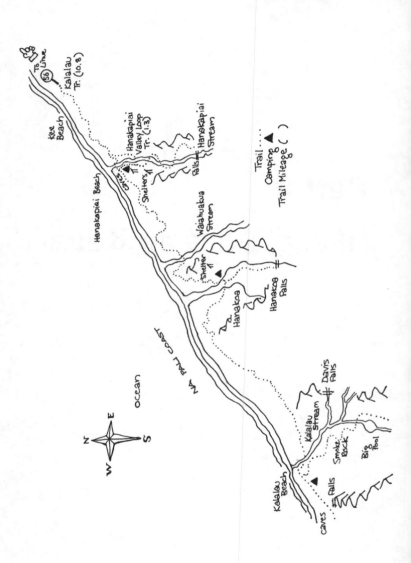

KALALAU TRAIL

(Hiking Area No. 1)

Rating: See individual hikes.

Features: Wilderness area, views, fruits, waterfalls, swimming, historical sites.

Permission: Camping permits are required for Hanakapiai, Hanakoa and Kalalau valleys. Permits for camping must be obtained from the Division of State Parks (see Appendix).

Hiking Distance & Time: See individual hikes.

Driving Instructions: 38 miles, 1 hour from Lihue. North on Route 56 to road's end.

Introductory Notes: When people talk about hiking on Kauai, they talk about visiting the uninhabited valleys of the Na Pali (the cliffs) Coast as evidenced by the comments registered by hikers on the sign-in at the trailhead—for example, "fantastic," "incredible," "Paradise," "the most beautiful place in the world." Kalalau ("the straying") trail to the end of the beach (10.8 miles) is the most exciting hike on the island. Until recently Kalalau Valley was part of the Makaweli ("fearful features") Ranch, which is owned by the Robinson family. The valley, the beach, and the Na Pali coastal lands now have state-park status and are under the jurisdiction and management of the Hawaii Department of Land and Natural Resources, Division of State Parks.

Few who have hiked the Kalalau Trail will deny its grandeur and its captivating allure. Cliffs rise precipitously above the blue-green water and the rugged, rocky north shore of Kauai. The valleys of the Na Pali Coast are accessible only by foot or by boat, and only during the summer when the tides expose a generous sandy beach, which is ripped away each year by winter storms. In the summer of 1981, the trail

Helicopter shuttle to Kalalau

was in good condition except for the area between the 3- and 6-mile markers. Numerous slides and fallen trees made the trail there quite hazardous, but passable with caution.

Special Instructions: Hiking the whole trail to Kalalau requires backpacking equipment for a comfortable, safe trip. Sound hiking boots are essential, since a good deal of your hiking is on soft cinders and ash along the precipitous coast and on rocky trail in the valleys. A strong, waterproof tent is needed to stand up under the wind at Kalalau and the rain at Hanakoa. Although fresh water is available all along the trail, you should boil the water or purify it with Halazone: people, goats and pigs are using the same stream. A light sleeping bag is adequate, particularly during the summer months when the nighttime temperature is very comfortable. Little if any clothing is necessary during the day, and it is common to find both sexes hiking without any. A backpacking stove is recommended since dry firewood is difficult to find and tree cutting is not permitted. The trailhead for the Kalalau Trail is at the end of the road, where it is possible to park your car. A word of caution, however, may save some grief: in recent years a number of break-ins have been reported, so don't leave anything in the car, and leave it unlocked.

A state park ranger is in residence in Kalalau. He does check for permits, in addition to his other duties.

On the Trail: Kee Beach to Hanakapiai Beach, 2 miles, 1 hour (trail rating: hardy family).

The trek to Hanakapiai (lit., "bay sprinkling food") Beach is an honest hike, it is one steep mile up and one steep mile down from Kee (lit., "avoidance")

Register at start of Kalalau Trail

Beach. This is a much frequented trail because tourist publications promise a verdant valley resplendent with native and introduced flora. No one is disappointed. Particularly abundant is the hala (*Pandanus tectorius*), an indigenous tree that grows in coastal areas. It is sometimes called "tourist pineapple," since the fruit resembles a pineapple and is jokingly identified as such by locals for tourists. Humor aside, the hala has been a valuable resource, the hollow trunk of the female tree being used as a pipe for drainage between taro patches. The leaves have commercial value, being used for weaving many items such as baskets, mats and hats—hats being particularly popular with tourists.

The first half mile up the cliff provides views at a couple of points back to Kee Beach and Haena ("wilderness") reefs. This part of the trail is usually shady because of the large trees and cool because of the trade winds and periodic rain showers. One source of shade is the large kukui (*Aleurites moluccana*) tree from which a beautiful and popular lei is made. To make a lei, each nut must be sanded, filed and

Hala tree—"tourist pineapple"

On the trail to Hanakapiai Beach

polished to a brilliant luster that is acquired from its own oil. Until the advent of electricity, kukui-nut oil was burned for light. Nicknamed the "candlenut tree" its trunk was shaped into canoes by early Hawaiians.

A wide, well-maintained trail leads up and down from the ½ to the 1¼ mile marker. With any luck you may find some sweet guava (*Psidium guajava*), a small yellow, lemon-sized fruit that is perhaps better in juice or jam form. Before eating one break it open and check for worms. They are tiny and are a little hard to see but are common in wild guava.

Near the 1-mile marker, look for a small springlet that flows year round and provides a thirst-quenching drink. At the 1½-mile marker, you'll have your first view of Hanakapiai Beach below, with its generous beach (during the summer months) and its crashing surf. Look for wild orchids, with their delicate purplish flowers, thriving along the banks of the trail.

On your descent to the beach, about three-quarters of the way down, the Hanakapiai Loop Trail goes left. It is 2 miles to the base of Hanakapiai Falls. You may continue on to the beach and take the west side of the loop into the valley. I suggest that you hike to the falls in the afternoon after a swim in the ocean or in the pools in Hanakapiai Stream. It is more likely to be warm and sunny in the valley and free of rain in the afternoon.

If you want to stay overnight at Hanakapiai Beach, you have a choice of campsites. There is a camping area on the beach along either side of the stream, and there are two Division of Forestry trail-crew shelters on the west side of the stream about ¼ and ¾ mile from the beach. Additionally, a number of large mango trees provide an idyllic and private campsite also on the west side off the loop trail. At low tide during the summer, you may prefer the unique experience of one of the cave campsites that are located on both the west and east sides of the beach. From Hanakapiai to Kalalau, you can expect considerable nudity. Indeed, you're pretty straight or different—depending on your point of view—if you're wearing clothes. Certainly the climate and the Eden-like setting seem to free one of any inhibitions he may have. You'll discover that there are a lot of healthy people on Kauai!

Hibiscus

Camping at Hanakapiai Beach

Hanakapiai Valley Loop Trail, 1.3 miles, 1 hour (trail rating: hardy family).

The Hanakapiai Valley loop is an easy hike along the stream and through a rain forest resplendent with native flora. The beginning of the trail on the west side of the valley contains some of the largest mango (*Mangifera indica*) trees anywhere. One grove surrounding the remains of a coffee mill contains a tree that is 23 feet in circumference. Obviously, it makes a shady sheltered campsite. The mango tree is not native to Hawaii, but its many varieties have done well there, and are popular with locals and tourists. However, the trees in this valley do not bear as well as those in drier areas because of a fungus that kills the blossoms in wet areas. Many people regard the mango fruit as second to none in taste and appearance.

The stone-wall enclosures are the remains of ancient taro terraces where the taro plant was grown to provide Hawaiians with their staple, poi. Hundreds of varieties of taro have been recorded from which poi, a thick paste, is produced. Poi is made from the tubers (roots), which are baked or boiled and then pounded by hand or machine. It may be eaten fresh or allowed to ferment for a few days, which adds a pleasant sour taste. Poi is traditionally eaten with the fingers along with pork or fish.

"Okolehau" ("okole" is translated "anus" or "buttocks"; and "hau" can mean "cool.") is a Division of Forestry trail-crew shelter near the coffee mill which you may use when it is not occupied by a trail crew.

At the ½ mile marker the loop trail turns left to cross the stream and return to the beach. It is a little wetter on the east side and the trail is more difficult to follow since it is overgrown with a variety of flora, including both common and strawberry guava fruit; ti, whose leaves provide hula dancers with their skirts; coffee with tiny green or red berries; and the beautiful

fragrant, delicate ginger. Continue on to the main
trail and return to the beach for a swim in the ocean
or in the freshwater pools in the stream.

**Hanakapiai Falls Trail from Hanakapiai Valley Loop
Trail, 1.3 miles, 1½ hours (trail rating: strenuous).**
   The hike to the falls is a must not only because the
falls are spectacular, but also because much serenity
and enchantment are to be found in the valley. The
first ¼ mile is an easy trail that snakes along the
stream. If the steam is high or if it is raining hard, you
should not attempt to hike to the falls, for the trail
narrows considerably in the upper portions and flash
flooding is a serious consideration. Just before the ¾
mile marker you cross the stream. If the crossing is
difficult due to high water, that is a good clue that
you should not continue until the water has receded.
At this crossing, the trail continues on the opposite
bank. You will make three stream crossings. The trail
is always easy to find because the valley is so narrow.
In this lower area, there are traces of abandoned taro
terraces. The last ½ mile is the most difficult part,
but perhaps the most enchanting, with inviting pools
and slides and verdant growth. The trail is cut along
the walls of the canyon in a number of places. Caution is well-advised. Although the pool at the base of
the falls is inviting, caution is again advised for there
is danger from falling rocks from the cliffs and the
ledge above the falls. Hanakapiai Falls cascades and
falls about 300 feet in the back of a natural amphi-
theater. You don't need to be told to swim and enjoy
the pools and the surrounding area. You will find safe
pools away from falling rocks.

Hanakapiai to Hanakoa, 4 miles, 2½ hours (trail rating: strenuous).

Serious hiking on the trail to Kalalau begins at this point as the trail climbs out of Hanakapiai Valley on a series of switchbacks for one mile. Hiking here in the morning means that the sun will be at your back and, with the trade wind, it should be relatively cool. The trail does not drop to sea level again until Kalalau Beach, some nine miles along the cliffs.

There are two small valleys before Hanakoa. The first is Hoolulu (lit., "to lie in sheltered waters"), which is first viewed from a cut in the mountain at the 3¼-mile marker. From here you descend to cross the valley and climb the opposite side. Hoolulu is thickly foliated with native and introduced plants that are typical of most valleys on the island. Ti, guava, morning glory, mountain orchids, and different kinds of ferns can be identified along with the larger kukui, koa and hala trees. Be careful at points where the trail narrows along a precipitous slope. In 1981 there were numerous slides across the trail and parts of the trail were heavily overgrown between the 3¼ and 5¾ mile markers. There is also a danger of falling rocks.

Waiahuakua Valley, at the 4¼-mile marker, is broader than Hoolulu. In August, with any luck, you are likely to find delicious ohia ai (*Eugenia malaccensis*), or mountain apples, growing along the trail. Abundant in Waiahuakua, these trees have smooth, dark green leaves and some attain a height of 50 feet. The fruit is a small red or pinkish apple with a thin, waxen skin, while the meat is flesh-white, crisp and juicy, with a large brown seed in the center—a very tasty repast for those lucky enough to find some. Additionally, the valley abounds in coffee, ti, guava, kukui, and mango.

At the 5¾-mile marker, you get your first view of Hanakoa (lit., "bay of koa trees or of warriors")

Valley which is a broad-terraced valley that was once cultivated by Hawaiians. Many of the terraced areas provide relatively sheltered camping sites. In addition, "Mango Shelter" has a roof-and-table camp and "Hanakoa Shack," a short distance away, is a Division of Forestry trail-crew shelter that is open to hikers when not in use by crews. Both are located along the trail a short distance into the valley. Camping in Hanakoa is quite an experience since it receives frequent rains, and as soon as you dry out, it rains again. However, the afternoon can be warm and sunny, just perfect for a swim in one of the many pools in the stream and a sunbath on the large, warm rocks along the bank. These are a favorite of nude sun worshippers.

To Hanakoa Falls, .4 mile, ¼ hour (trail rating: strenuous).

Extreme caution should be exercised when hiking to Hanakoa Falls. A 40-foot section of the cliff recently slid 200 feet to the rocky streambed. The trail begins between the stream crossing and the 6½-mile marker and passes a wilderness campsite. If you plan to camp in Hanakoa, you should be prepared for a lot of rain, wetness and humidity. To compensate, you will have solitude and your own private swimming pool.

Hanakoa to Kalalau Beach, 4.8 miles, 3 hours (trail rating: strenuous).

Your physical condition and your hiking skill will be tested on this, the most difficult part of the Kalalau Trail. Not only is most of the hiking on switchbacks that alternate up and down along a very precipitous cliff, but also the danger is increased by a number of slides along the trail. Another hazard is the hot afternoon sun unless you begin hiking early. However, the rewards are great. Indeed, the views of the northwest coastline are absolutely breathtaking and staggeringly beautiful. It is difficult to think of

Cliffs along Kalalau Trail

another view in the world that compares.

At the 6½-mile marker, you enter land that until 1975 was part of the Makaweli (lit., "fearful features") cattle ranch. The area becomes increasingly dry as you continue west, and only the smaller more arid types of vegetation survive, like sisal and lantana. Lantana (*Lantana camara*) is a popular flower that blossoms almost continuously. Its flowers vary in color from yellow to orange to pink to red; infrequently, they are white with a yellow center. If you hike in the early morning or late afternoon you're likely to frighten feral goats foraging near the trail and near some of the small streams along the trail.

Although there are only a few trail-mileage markers over the rest of the route, there is no chance of getting lost. The trail is over open land and visible ahead. There are at least five reliable sources of water between Hanakoa and Kalalau. The admonition to treat or to boil water applies.

Pohakuao (lit., "day stone") is the last small valley before Kalalau. As you ascend the west side of Pohakuao along a pali with sparse foliage and reddish earth, you get your first view of Kalalau, a welcome sight after a difficult three miles from Hanakoa. There is no mistaking Kalalau, for it is a large, broad valley some two miles wide and three miles long. From the ridge, a precipitous snake-like trail drops abruptly to Kalalau Stream where a rushing creek and cool pools await the weary hiker.

Camping is allowed only on the beach, in the trees fronting the beach and in the caves at the far end of the beach. Try to find a spot that will shelter you from the strong winds and the hot daytime sun. Some campers find shelter in the low scrub along the beach during the day and then sleep on the beach during the cool and usually wind-free nights. Lantana and common guava are particularly abundant along the trail in the beach area. You should easily find some ripe

guava to add to your meals. Don't drink the stream
water until you boil or treat it. The falls at the end of
the beach by the caves is your best bet for safe water
although it would probably be a good idea to boil or
to treat the water also. The water from the falls also
serves the feral goats that you will undoubtedly see in
the morning or at dusk when they visit to refresh
themselves. The falls also make for a pleasant shower,
with a small bathing pool at the base.

Kalalau Beach to Big Pool, 2 miles one way, 1½ hour.

The best trail into the valley begins on the west
side of Kalalau Stream at the marked trailhead. Before
heading into the valley, hike to the top of the knoll
above the beach, also on the west side of the stream.
The remains of a heiau—a pre-Christian place of worship—lie between the knoll and the beach and are
clearly identifiable from this vantage point. Little is
known about this nameless heiau. Remember that
such places are still revered by many people, and a
rock wrapped in a ti leaf and left on a heiau site is
believed to protect the traveler.

From the trailhead, the trail parallels the stream
for a short distance and then ascends an eroded rise.
From here the trail alternately passes open and forested areas. In the wooded areas look for oranges,
mango, common guava and rose apple. Each is common in the valley and can supplement a backpackers
diet. At the one-mile point, Smoke Rock is a convenient place to pause in an open area from which the
entire valley can be viewed. This is the place where
the valley marijuana growers and residents used to
meet to smoke and to talk stories. The rest of the
trail to Big Pool is under the shade of giant mango and
rose apple trees. Before reaching Big Pool, a side
stream crossing must be made. Our trail then meets a
trail which to the left leads to Kalalau Stream and to
the beach, and to the right leads to Big Pool. Heading
into the valley, the next stream crossing is Kalalau

Honopu Beach

Stream. Big Pool, a short distance from this crossing, is easily identified. Two room-sized pools are separated by a natural water slide which is a joy to slip down into the cool water below. It is a "relatively" smooth slide!

Kalalau Beach to Davis Falls, 1 mile from Big Pool.

In 1984 a group of island Boy Scouts and Explorer Scouts cut a trail from the stream near Big Pool to Davis Falls. The trailhead is at a point just above the last major stream crossing before Big Pool, and it is posted "Davis Falls 0.9 miles." The trail passes through heavy brush until it reaches a pool at the base of the upper falls. The falls are named for Richard Davis, an outdoorsman who has explored the valley for many years. The falls are a marvelous place to swim or shower and to pause to enjoy the sights and smells of Kalalau, Kauai's most precious treasure.

Kalalau abounds in a variety of life. Beach naupaka (*Scaevola frutescens*), with small, fragrant, white flowers, can be found near the beach, mixed with the low sisal and lantana. Hala, ti, ferns, bamboo, bananas, mango, kukui, monkeypod and many other species of flora can be identified. Rock terraces where Hawaiians planted taro as late as the 1920s are also common.

Some very daring people attempt to wade and swim around the point where the beach ends on the west side in an effort to visit Honopu (lit., "conch bay") Valley, the so-called "Valley of the Lost Tribe" —a reference to the legendary little people named Mu who once lived there. Interestingly, the remains of an ancient settlement have been found in the valley. We don't know who left them, but there's no evidence it was the Mu people. However, the swim around the point takes about 15 minutes and is very risky due to the strong current and undertow in the ocean. If you must see Honopu Valley, better charter a boat or a helicopter in Lihue.

Locals and visitors enjoy speculating about the exploits and the hideouts of Kalalau's most famous citizen, Koolau. Commonly called "Koolau the Leper," this native Hawaiian was born in Kekaha in 1862. Three years after showing signs of leprosy, at the age of 27, Koolau and the other lepers of Kauai were ordered to the leper colony on Molokai, and were promised that their wives and children could accompany them. When the ship sailed without his wife and child, Koolau, realizing he had been tricked, dove overboard and swam ashore. Together with his wife and child he made the perilous descent into Kalalau Valley to join other lepers who sought to escape deportation. A year later, local authorities decided to round up the lepers, all of whom agreed to go to Molokai except Koolau. A sheriff's posse exchanged fire with Koolau, who shot and killed a deputy. Martial law was declared, and a detachment of the national guard was sent from Honolulu

with orders to get their man dead or alive. A small
cannon was mounted near the site where Koolau was
thought to be hiding. In the ensuing "battle" Koolau
shot two guardsmen and one accidentally shot and
killed himself fleeing the leper. The remaining guardsmen fled from the valley to the beach. In the morning
they blasted Koolau's hideout with their cannon. Be-
lieving him dead, the guardsmen left the valley. But
Koolau had moved his family the night before the
cannonading, and they lived in the valley for about
five more years, always fearful that the guard was
still looking for him. They hid during the day and
hunted for food at night. Tragically, their son de-
veloped signs of leprosy and soon died; a year later,
the dread disease claimed Koolau. Piilani, his wife,
buried her husband in the valley that had become
their home along with his gun which had enabled
them to be together to the end.

To some, Koolau is a folk hero who received unfair
treatment by the government. Indeed, locals claim
that Koolau frequently left his valley hideout to visit
friends and relatives on Kauai. Whatever the facts,
it makes for an intersting story and campfire con-
versation.

LUMAHAI BEACH

(Hiking Area No. 2)

Rating: Family.

Features: Swimming beach, picnic, views.

Permission: None.

Hiking Distance & Time: .2 miles, 10 minutes.

Driving Instructions: 33 miles, ¾ hour from Lihue. North on Route 56 past Hanalei, park by sign *Lumahai Beach*.

Introductory Notes: Lumahai (lit., "a certain twist of the fingers in making string figures") Beach really doesn't qualify as a hike, but should be included in any visit to Kauai. Lumahai is regarded as perhaps the most beautiful beach on the Islands; certainly it is the most photographed, appearing in tourist papers and on calendars throughout the world. It has also appeared in many movies, most notably "South Pacific."

On the Trail: The Hawaiian Visitor's Bureau sign identifies the trail to the beach at a curve past the town of Hanalei. Park off the road and if possible remove all valuables from your car. Unfortunately, even locked cars have not stopped thieves. If you remove your valuables, leave the windows open and car unlocked to avoid damage.

The trail dops about 50 feet and passes through a pandanus grove to the beach. Under the shade of the hala, or screwpine (*Pandanus odoratissimus*), is an idyllic spot to picnic. As previously noted, the hala is frequently called "tourist pineapple" since the fruit somewhat resembles a pineapple and it is jokingly identified as such to tourists by locals. The fruit is sometimes cut into sections, which are then strung to make a fruit lei. The leaves, called lauhala, are dried and woven into mats and hats which are popular for beach and casual wear.

Swimming should be approached with some caution due to the strong offshore currents. If you follow the rock-laden shore around the east side of the beach, you have a panorama of Hanalei Bay and the Princeville development on the far eastern cliff.

Lumahai Beach

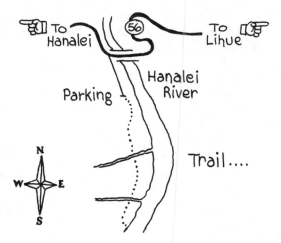

HANALEI RIVER

(Hiking Area No. 3)

Rating: Family.

Features: Swimming, bamboo forest, fruits.

Permission: None.

Hiking Distance & Time: 1.3 miles, ¾ hour.

Driving Instructions: 31 miles, ¾ hour from Lihue. North on Route 56 (29.3 miles), then left on road after crossing the bridge in Hanalei Valley. Drive to road's end (1.9 miles) and park by the Dept. of Land & Natural Resources sign.

Introductory Notes: The Hanalai (lit., "crescent bay") area is rich in history, having been a large Hawaiian community where taro was grown to support the population. Later, many Chinese settlers came to cultivate rice in the valley. During the missionary period numerous experiments were conducted in efforts to cultivate coffee, silk, cotton and oranges. Oranges were once shipped to California, where they had commercial value until oranges began to be grown there. During the 1850's the harbor area was an important port for whaling and trading ships. Rice, taro and cattle were exported.

A hike into the valley is a pleasant, cool trek through an area rich in native and introduced plants with a generous variety of fruits to enjoy during your trip.

On the Trail: As you approach the trailhead, you are passing through taro fields that have been cultivated for many years. The route follows a jeep road used by hunters. In the early morning it is common to meet pig hunters with their dogs hunting the small pig which is a popular sport with locals. A number of large mango trees border the road. Also look for oranges, guavas and delicious pomelo (*Citrus maxima*) tree which yields a large cantaloupe-sized fruit that has the aroma and taste of both grapefruit and orange. Both locals and tourists seek out these tasty treats, so the pickings are sometimes lean. Additionally, you will find a variety of flowers, particularly the small, delicate, purple mountain orchid and the aromatic ginger. Yellow ginger (*Zingiber zerumbet*) is prolific along the road, and is easy to identify by the delicately fragrant, light yellow blossom that rises at the end of a narrow tube just behind an olive-colored bract. The leaves are a luxuriant green. They make a lovely and popular lei.

Bear to the left off the end of the road, pass through a gate in the fence and follow the trail to the first of two streams that enter the river. A small but magnificent bamboo forest surrounds you, and a cacophony of sounds is heard when the wind rushes through the dense growth. Bamboo has long been an important product on the Islands, having been used for fuel, furniture, musical instruments, utensils, building material and paper. And bamboo sprouts are commonly eaten on the Islands as a vegetable.

Shortly, you cross another stream and go through another bamboo forest with the river a short distance beyond. A number of large mango trees along the river create a delightful place to picnic and from which to dive into the river for a refreshing swim. From the river it is possible to hike along the banks into the interior, but you will be crossing private land and may not be welcome.

Hanalei Valley

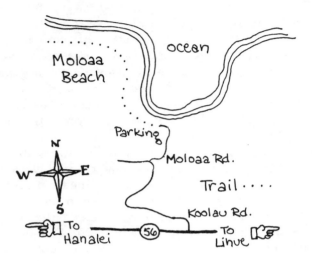

MOLOAA BEACH

(Hiking Area No. 4)

Rating: Family.

Features: Swimming, shells, fishing, fruits, views.

Permission: None.

Hiking Distance & Time: 1.5 miles, 1 hour.

Driving Instructions: 18 miles, ½ hour from Lihue. North on Route 56 for 16.6 miles, right on Koolau Road for 1.2 miles, and right on Moloaa Road to end. Park along beach right-of-way.

Introductory Notes: The Moloaa (lit., "matted roots" —said to be of the paper mulberry growing here) Beach hike is included here because it is one of the more secluded beaches on the island—a place where you can explore, fish, hunt for shells, or swim without intrusion. Check the mango trees along Moloaa Road for ripe fruit. Unfortunately most of the fruit is out of reach unless you have a fruit picker—a bamboo pole with a cloth basket attached to a loop at one end. Many locals carry a pole that can be extended like a fishing rod and folded when not in use.

If you drive Moloaa Road at night, perhaps you shouldn't carry fresh pork. Even some present-day Hawaiians believe that the Demigod Kamapuaa, who is part pig, part man, still lives in the valley and will assume a variety of shapes and attack if he smells fresh pork. He can be outwitted, however, if the meat is wrapped in ti leaves.

On the Trail: You might hike the beach in search of shells or, with some luck, you might find a glass-ball float used by Japanese fishermen on their nets. Some break loose and make the long journey to Kauai.

The trail along the northwest side of the bay, a fisherman's trail, leads to some of the best spots from which to cast. Usually you need to walk out on the coral. Before you do, however, sit on the bank a while and watch the ocean to study the surf conditions. The only company you are likely to have is an occassional fisherman or the cattle or horses that graze on the slopes.

On the upper slopes you can identify the paper mulberry (*Broussonetia papyrifera*) from which the name of the area is derived. It is a small tree with lobed leaves covered with woolly hairs on the undersides of the leaves. The bark of the plant was an important source of tapa, the cloth of ancient Hawaii. Tapa was made by removing the outer bark of the tree and soaking and beating the inner bark. A carved wooden mallet was used to pound the fibers until they became thin and flexible. Sheets were joined by the same pounding process, usually performed by men, while the women would decorate the cloth using a block printing method or leaves dipped in dye and pressed on the cloth.

The trail on the east side of the bay also snakes along the coast and provides a number of places to fish, picnic or simply enjoy the solitude.

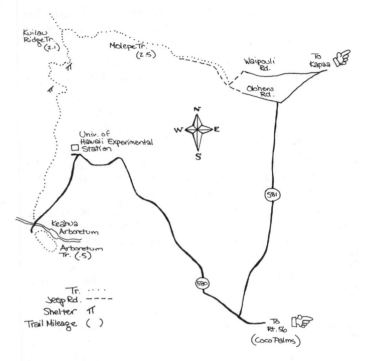

KEAHUA TRAILS

(Hiking Area No. 5)

Rating: See individual hikes.

Features: Swimming hole, native and introduced plants, fruits.

Permissions: None.

Hiking Distance & Time: See individual hikes.

Driving Instructions:

to Keahua Arboretum and Kuilau trails 12 miles, ½ hour from Lihue.

North on Route 56, left on Route 580 to University of Hawaii Agriculture Experiment Station, left on paved road (1.8 miles) to Keahua Stream. Kuilau Ridge Trailhead is on the right at a small turnout just before the stream and Keahua Arboretum Trailhead is on the left just past the stream opposite a large parking area.

to Moalepe Trail 12 miles, ½ hour from Lihue.
North from Lihue on Route 56, left on Route 580, right on Route 581, for 1.6 miles, left on Olohena Road for 1.6 miles to pavement end and intersection with Waipouli Road. Park on shoulder of road.

Introductory Notes: The three hiking trails in the Keahua area offer some pleasurable experiences. They offer some marvelous views of the eastside coastline and of the Makaleha Mountains. Since the Moalepe Trail intersects the Kuilau Ridge Trail, you have an opportunity to follow the latter trail to Keahua Arboretum.

Keahua Arboretum, .5 miles, ½ hour, (hike rating: family).

Keahua (lit., "the mound") Arboretum is a project of the Hawaii State Department of Land and Natural Resources, Division of Forestry. Here is a good chance to view a variety of native and introduced plants and

Ohia lehua blossom

to swim in a cool, fresh-water pool. The arboretum receives an annual average rainfall of 95 inches. The State Forest Reserve area extends west to the top of Mt. Waialeale ("overflowing water"), the highest spot on Kauai and the wettest place on earth, with an average annual rainfall of 468 inches. It once received a record 628 inches!

The trail follows a series of numbered posts that correspond with the numbers and narrative in a leaflet offered by the Division of Forestry, *A Trailside Guide to the Keahua Forestry Arboretum.*

"1. EARLY POLYNESIAN PLANT IMPORTS

"Early Polynesian settlers are credited with introducing twenty-four plants to Hawaii approximately 1,000 years ago. Several specimens of these plant species may be seen in the Keahua Arboretum. Two of them are kukui (*Aleurites moluccana*) and milo (*Thespesia populnea*). Three kukui trees are growing across the road at the edge of the parking area. A group of milo trees has been planted on the arboretum side of the road near the stream. Kukui trees, also called candlenut trees, had several uses. The most noteworthy use was the burning of its oily nuts for a light source. Kukui is Hawaii's State Tree. Today, as in old Hawaii, the wood of the milo tree is priced for its use in making beautiful umekes, or calabashes.

"2. LUMBER TREES

"The trees with the colorful bark are painted gum (*Eucalyptus deglupta*). This tree species is native to the Philippines and New Guinea. It starts life from a very tiny seed. The seeds that are produced in the pods of this tree number over a million seeds per pound.

"The less colorful barked trees behing the painted gum trees are rose gum (*Eucalyptus grandis*) from Australia. Both of these trees are lumber-producing species.

"3. WATER FOR POWER AND DRINKING

"Forest reserves are managed to provide many benefits. Their most important benefit in Hawaii is water supply. The Hawaii Legislature, as early as 1876, passed a law to prevent forest destruction and the consequence of diminishing water supply.

"The Makaleha mountains, viewed through the scope on the right, are the source watershed for the domestic water supply for homes in the Wailua and Kapaa Homestead area. Rain falling on the mountains percolates into the soil and is collected in tunnels for distribution into the county water system. Good forest cover increases infiltration of water into the soil. This not only helps to increase ground water supply but it also helps prevent soil erosion and floods caused by surface run-off.

"The scope on the left is aimed at the ridge that forms a saddle and is the drainage divide between Hanalei and Wailua. Many years ago Hawaiian trails crossed the saddle to provide access between north and south Kauai.

"4. HAU

"Preparation for planting in this entire arboretum required removal of a dense tangle of hau (*Hibiscus tiliaceus*). An example of the original condition of the arboretum area can be studied inside the short "Hau Tunnel Trail." This yellow-flowered hibiscus was an early Hawaiian introduced plant.

"5. GOOD COVER—CLEAN STREAMS

"Trees and plants protect the streams. Notice how roots bind the soil and hold it in place. When stream banks are washed away, mud and silt cover the bottom of the stream. Observe the soil structure across the stream. This is alluvial material (a mixture of rocks and soil washed down from the mountains above), which was laid in place by flooding and erosion forces before a protective plant cover was well established in the watershed.

"6. OHIA LEHUA

"The tree at this marker is an ohia lehua (*Metrosideros collina*). It is the most common native tree species in Hawaii. Early Hawaiian uses for the wood of ohia included house timbers, poi boards, idols and kapa beaters. In the early 1900's, railroad ties hewn from ohia logs were exported for use on the mainland.

"Land across the stream, cleared of hau in 1973, is being planted to many tree species from all over the world. Some of these trees will provide the Division of Forestry with seeds for planting in other areas.

"7. STREAM-ASSOCIATED WILDLIFE

"Unpolluted streams benefit wildlife. Streams in this forest reserve provide a home for native and introduced fish. The native Hawaiian Oopu lives here, but their population is reduced from what it was years ago. Smallmouth bass provide good fishing in the streams in this area.

"Tahitian prawn, a fresh-water prawn that goes to sea in its larva, or baby, stage, is a good example of the ability of some introduced organisms to establish, spread and multiply. Tahitian prawns were planted by the Division of Fish and Game in a stream on the island of Molokai about 15 years ago. Tahitian prawns, esteemed as a delicious food, are found in this stream and other streams on Kauai, established here as a result of the ocean-going larvae from the Molokai release.

"The native Koloa duck is the most noteworthy bird for which these streams provide an important habitat.

"The two mango trees across the streams were planted many years ago. Mango trees were first introduced to Hawaii in 1824.

"8. IRRIGATION WATER

"The left fork of the trail at this marker leads

through a young monkey pod (*Pithecellobium saman*) grove. This trail leads to a geological survey stream-gaging station that was established in 1912. Forested watersheds provide a sustained water resource for irrigation of agricultural crops in the farming areas makai [toward the sea].

"Return to post number 8 and continue on the trail up the hill.

"As you climb the trail, at the second switchback, notice the native hala tree (*Pandanus tectorius*) with its stiltlike trunk. Lauhala, the leaves of hala trees, are important today for making rugs, purses, baskets, mats and hats. The early Hawaiians also made many uses of hala trees.

"9. BRUSH ESTABLISHMENT AND CONTROL

"Aggressive noxious plants quickly invade and occupy forest lands following a fire in high rainfall areas. If they are not controlled, they smother and choke out native plants and destroy many wildland uses and value potentials. Beneficial tree and ground covers can be planted that can combat the takeover of this noxious brush.

"The scope is aimed at one of many Norfolk Island pine (*Araucaria heterophylla*) trees that were planted on a section of the forest reserve after a forest fire occurred in 1971. When the Norfolk Island pine trees grow older and larger, their branches will create shade and suppress the dense underbrush, which consists of lantana and melestoma.

"10. MELESTOMA, THE SCOURGE OF EAST KAUAI

"The understory (plants under the tree canopy) is composed of malabar melestoma (*Melestoma melbathricum*). This pink-flowered plant from India was introduced at Kauai as a yard plant. Birds have spread the seed into forest reserves, causing its permanent establishment into dense thickets impenetrable by

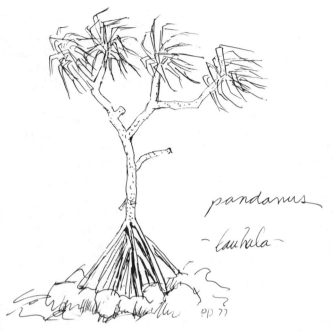

pandanus
- lauhala -

pp 77

man or beast. Tree planting and understory plant alteration forest management practices can improve the use value of weed-infested forests for recreation and other forest values.

"The tree cover on this site is *Eucalyptus saligna*, planted in 1968, after the area was cleared by bulldozer. This tree is a fast-growing lumber species from Australia. In this area, its ability to grow rapidly is essential for it to survive the early competition of the melestoma. Due to its light branching characteristic, this eucalyptus does not produce enough shade to completely stop the growth of the melestoma, but it does reduce its vigor for other control methods. On your right is a sample of the same tree planting where the melestoma understory is being replaced with a ground cover of grass. The tree shade and grass combination will prevent reestablishment of the melestoma.

"11. NATIVE PLANTS

"There are over 1,800 species of plants native to the Hawaiian Islands. Most of them are endemic (found no where else in the world). Competition of aggressive introduced plants is having a devastating effect on the natives.

"Forest management practices can improve sites for native plant establishment in problem areas by mixing compatible introduced and native species. Three native plants endemic to Kauai have been planted at this site: to the right of the post is a *Kokia kauaiensis*, a beautiful red-flowering tree; to the left of the post are Kokio keokeo (*Hibiscus waimeae*), a white-flowering hibiscus; and across the trail behind you is Rocks' hibiscus (*Hibiscus rockii*), a yellow-flowering hibiscus.

"12. CONIFERS

"No conifers (pinelike evergreen trees) are native to Hawaii. Many species however, have been introduced during the past two hundred years. Two species of conifers have been planted near this stop. To the right of the marker is an Australian Kauri (*Agathis robusta*). The sharp-leaved trees to the left of the post are parana pine (*Araucaria angustifolia*), a lumber species from Brazil. Trees of the Araucaria family were much more prevalent over the world many years ago. Though there are no species representative of this family native to mainland U.S.A. today, petrified specimens reveal that a mainland species was very common in Arizona approximately 160 million years ago."

Be certain to return to the stream for a swim. There is usually a rope suspended from the mango tree on the bank about 100 yards from the shelter. It's a fun place.

taro

Moalepe Trail, 2.5 miles, 1½ hours (hike rating: hardy family). Elevation gain 500 feet.

On the Trail: Do not attempt to drive beyond the Olohena-Waipouli Road intersection because the road is deeply rutted and, when wet, very slippery. The first part of the trail is on a right-of-way dirt road over pasture land. The usually cloud-enshrouded Makaleha (lit., "eyes looking about as in wonder and admiration") Mountains rise majestically to the northwest. In fact, the State of Hawaii, Division of Forestry, which is in charge of the area, has plans to extend the trail to the top of the Makalehas. Be sure to pause to enjoy the panorama of the coastline, from Moloaa on the north to Lihue on the south. There are some guavas along the fence and even more in the pasture, which is private land. The trail is a popular equestrian route with riders who rent horses from the ranches in the area: evidence of this fact can be found on the trail!

The first mile is a gentle ascent in open country.
Then the trail enters the forest reserve. Hereafter, the
trail is bordered with a variety of plants and trees, including the wild, or Philippine, orchid, different types
of ferns, eucalyptus trees and the popular ohia lehua,
with its pretty red blossoms. In the forest reserve the
road-trail narrows and begins to twist and turn along
the ridge, with many small and heavily foliated
gulches to the left and Moalepe (lit., "chick with
comb") Valley to the right. You can expect rain and
therefore a muddy trail to the end of the hike. The
trail reaches a junction with the Kuilau Ridge trail on
a flat, open area at the 2.1-mile point. The ridge trail
to the south (left) descends to two trail shelters and
eventually ends at Keahua Arboretum, 2.1 miles from
the junction. There is a sheltered picnic site 0.2 mile
south of the junction along the Kuilau Ridge Trail.
From the junction the Moalepe Trail is a footpath
that snakes northwestward for 0.4 mile along Kuilau
Ridge to a lookout point from which an enchanting
panorama awaits the hiker.

Kuilau Ridge Trail, 2.1 miles, 1½ hours (trail rating: hardy family).

One of the most scenic hiking trails on the island,
the Kuilau ("to string together leaves or grass") Ridge
Trail climbs the ridge from Keahua Arboretum to two
vista-point picnic sites. From the trailhead to trail's
end, an abundance of native and introduced plants
greets the hiker. The ascent of the ridge is on a well-
maintained foot and horse trail lined with hala, ti
plants, from which hula skirts are fashioned, and the
very pretty lavender wild, or Philippine, orchid. But
the best prize is a couple of mountain apple trees on
the left side of the trail a short distance up from the
trailhead. Perhaps you'll find some apples, which are
red or pink when ripe.

At the 1¼-mile point the trail reaches a large flat

area and a trail shelter and a picnic site. It is a delightful spot for a pause to enjoy views of the many gulches and the Makaleha Mountains beyond. However, if you plan to picnic, continue on for 0.8 mile to the second trail shelter and picnic area. The trail to the second shelter passes through one of the most beautiful places on the whole island. The Kuilau Ridge Trail twists and turns on a razorback ridge past a number of small waterfalls. It is a treasure to savor. Before reaching the shelter, the trail crosses a footbridge at the bottom of a gulch and then ascends the ridge to a large flat area and the picnic spot. From here, the trail continues 0.2 mile to its junction with the Moalepe Trail.

Frigate birds on Kauai

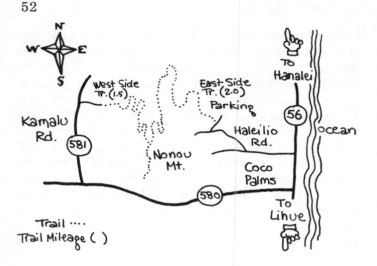

West Side Tr. (1.5)
East Side Tr. (2.0)
Parking
To Hanalei
Kamalu Rd.
581
56
ocean
Haleilio Rd.
Nonou Mt.
Coco Palms
580
To Lihue

Trail ····
Trail Mileage ( )

NONOU MOUNTAIN (SLEEPING GIANT)
(Hiking Area No. 6)

Rating: Hardy Family.

Features: Views of Kauai, fruits.

Permission: None.

Hiking Distance & Time: Consult individual hikes.

Driving Instructions:

East side—7 miles, ¼ hour from Lihue. North from Lihue on Route 56 past Coco Palms Hotel, left on Haleilio Road for 1.2 miles, park off road by sign *Nonou Trail.*

West side—10 miles, ½ hour from Lihue. North from Lihue on Route 56, left on Route 580, right on Route 581 (Kamalu Road) for 1.2 miles to trailhead sign *Nonou Trail* opposite 1055 Kamalu Road.

Introductory Notes: There are two routes to the summit of Nonou (lit., "throwing") mountain both of which are good, well-maintained trails that will take you to the giant's chin and to his forehead. Nonou is truly one of the best hikes on Kauai. Be sure to carry one quart of water, since it is a hot hike in spite of frequent trade winds.

It is told that the giant Puni lived among the legendary small folk, the Menehune, but was so clumsy that he continually knocked down their homes and their stone walls. Nevertheless, he was so friendly that the Menehune could not help but like him. One day the little people were faced with an invasion, and they went to the giant in the hope that he would destroy their enemies. However, they found him asleep on a ridge near Kapaa (lit., "the solid or the closing"). In an effort to awaken him, they threw large rocks on his stomach, which rebounded toward the ocean, destroying some of the invading canoes and causing the others to flee. In the morning they tried to awaken Puni again, only to discover that some of the rocks they had thrown at him had landed in his mouth. Tragically, he had swallowed them and died in his sleep.

Menehune fishpond, attributed to Hawaii's legendary elves.

On the Trail: East-side Trail, 2 miles, 1½ hours, 1,250 feet gain.

You can drive up the short access road to the water-filtration plant and park. The marked trailhead is across a drainage ditch.

The trail is a series of well-defined switchbacks along the northeast side of the mountain. DO NOT hike on the southeast side, for it is extremely dangerous and precipitous. Pause frequently and enjoy the vistas overlooking the east side of Kauai. Below you lie the Wailua Houselots, while the Wailua River and the world famous Coco Palm resort are to your front right. There are ¼ mile trail markers along the entire route.

The large trees that flourish in the area not only offer a relatively shady trail, but also provide some shelter from showers, which are common. You will find guava, ti, tree ferns, a variety of eucalyptus, and others that deserve special note.

The hau (*Hibiscus tiliaceus*) tree is of particular interest not because of its pretty bright-yellow blossom but because of its long, sinuous branches that interlock to form an impenetrable barrier. Locals jokingly note that the tree is appropriately named (hau, pronounced how) because where they are plentiful, no one knows "hau" to pass through!

On a spacious overlook at about the one-mile-point, you can rest in the shade of the ironwood (*Casuarina equisetifolia*) tree, which resembles a pine because of its long, slender, drooping, dull-green needles. It is an introduced tree that has a long life and is very useful as a windbreak or shade tree.

Just beyond the 1½ mile marker, the west-side trail merges with ours for the ascent to the summit. Alii (lit. "chief") Shelter and Table at the 1¾-mile marker is a pleasant place to picnic and to enjoy the panorama of the island and the solitude. There are a number of benches near the shelter that provide comfortable places to meditate. You should see a white-tailed tropic bird (*Phaethon lepturus*) as it soars along the mountain-side with its conspicuous 16-inch tail streamers.

From the shelter, walk south through the monkey-pod trees to survey the trail to the giant's "chin," "nose" and "forehead" that leads a short ½ mile to the summit. Look over the trail and judge your ability to walk across a narrow ridge above a nearly vertical 500-foot cliff, to scramble up about 50 feet on your hands and knees to the "chin" and to walk about 150 yards along a narrow ridge to the "forehead." In spite of the hazard, the views of the island are compensation.

West-side Trail, 1.5 miles, 1 hour, 1,000 feet gain.

The west-side trail is a bit shorter and not as steep, and offers more shade than the east-side trail. This trail passes by Queen's Acres and across a cattle range before entering the forest reserve. You will hike through a variety of introduced trees much like those found on the east side.

Look for the wild, or philippine, orchid (*Spathoglottis plicata*). The wild variety if usually lavender, with what appear to be five starlike petals, but are actually two petals and three sepals.

The trails join at the 1½ mile marker for the short trek to Alii Shelter and on to the summit.

Cliffs along Kalalau Trail

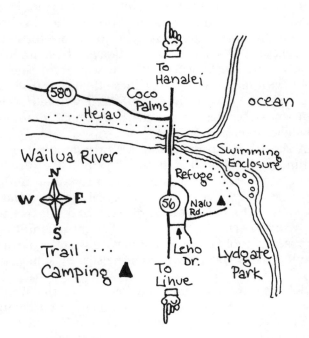

LYDGATE PARK

(Hiking Area No. 7)

Rating: Family.

Features: Swimming, a heiau, a place of refuge, picnicking, fruits.

Permission: None.

Hiking Distance & Time: 1 mile, 1 hour.

Driving Instructions: 6 miles, ¼ hour from Lihue. North from Lihue on Route 56, right on Leho Dr. at 5-mile marker, right on Nalu Road to parking by picnic area.

On the Trail: Lydgate has it all: hiking, wading, swimming, picnicking, and a bit of Hawaiiana. Begin your hike along the beach in front of the pavillion. If you begin at daybreak you may be fortunate enough to find some glass ball floats, which are highly prized by locals, who will even search for them at night with lanterns. Most of these floats are from the nets of the Japanese fishermen, so they have traveled thousands of miles. Some have been found more than 30 inches in circumference.

A short way north, the park's swimming enclosure is fun for children and the only safe place to swim. There are strong currents in this area, and an unusually heavy surf. Frequently, the local rescue squad is called to help swimmers in distress who fail to heed the warning signs on the beach. The most famous of all rescues took place a number of years ago when Frank Sinatra was pulled from the surf by some local boys.

Between the swimming enclosure and the Wailua (lit., "two waters") River are the remains of a Temple of Refuge, a place of importance in old Hawaii. Each island had a place of refuge where those who had been vanquished in battle, violators of tabus, and noncombatants could find safety from capture or punishment. These havens were respected by all. After a period of time and prayer, the individual could return home—a very humane concept and practice.

Occasionally, when the ocean currents remove the sand, petroglyphs are visible on a group of black rocks below the temple. Their significance and meaning remain a mystery.

From here it is a short hike over the bridge then across the river to Route 580 on the northside. The road goes between the river and the Coco Palms resort complex.

From the junction, follow the road for 0.2 mile to Holo-Holo-Ku (lit., "to run-and-stand") Heiau (a place of worship) on the left side of the road. Heiaus played an important part in pre-Christian Hawaiian culture. There are hundreds of known heiaus on the Islands that served specifically to ensure rain, good crops, or success in war, while others were used for human sacrifice. Here you'll find a large sacrificial stone forming the southwest corner of the heiau. As you stroll through the heiau bear in mind that it is a religious place and should be respected as such.

Other points of interest in the heiau are the royal birthstones, a priest's house, and reproductions of idols. The originals are to be found in the Bishop Museum in Honolulu. Royal birthstones were important in ancient Hawaii. Pregnant women in the royal family would visit a heiau to ensure the royal status of an unborn infant.

A large mango tree across the road may be checked for fresh fruit, although the mangoes may be inaccessible unless you have a picker.

Follow the sign to a small public cemetery behind the heiau which contains a number of lava headstones. Beyond the cemetery through the brush are a number of vistas which provide views of the river and the resort complex below.

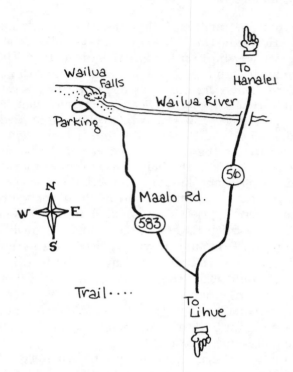

WAILUA FALLS

(Hiking Area No. 8)

Rating: Strenuous.

Features: Swimming hole, fruit, waterfall.

Permission: None.

Hiking Distance & Time: .5 miles, ½ hour.

Driving Instructions: 5 miles, 20 minutes from Lihue. North on Route 56, left on Route 583 (signed *Wailua Falls*) to end.

Introductory Notes: The power and beauty of Wailua (lit., "many waters") Falls after a heavy rain are awesome. Locals probably visit the falls as much as

Wailua Falls

do tourists. Periodically, some daring individual re-enacts the ancient practice of diving into the pool below from atop the falls. Hawaiian chiefs at one time would dive from the falls on a wager or to prove their courage.

On the Trail: The hike to the pool below the falls is short but not without some difficulty and hazard. An extremely steep trail descends from the road to the pool 0.2 mile before the guard rail at the end of the road. A large dirt turnout where you can park marks the point of the trailhead. When wet, which it usually is, the steep trail is very slippery and dangerous. The trail makes a rather abrupt drop to the stream below. Unless recent rains have swollen the stream, you can hike along the bank to the pool below the falls.

From the end of the road, a number of short trails take you to the top of the falls and to many pools in the stream. About 200 yards above the falls, just below a sugar-cane road, is a generous pool surrounded by large rocks from which you can dive and on which you can sun—an incomparable place for relaxation and solitude.

The remains of a narrow-gauge railroad bridge are located above the falls. Sugar cane was transported to the mill on this railroad before the introduction of the cane truck.

By now, you have probably spotted the mango trees along the road and above the stream on the south side. What a treat!

In 1985 a chain link fence and warning signs were placed at the end of the road to prevent people from getting to the top of the falls from which several people have fallen and one has been killed. It is safe to swim in the pools upstream from the falls, but keep away from the top.

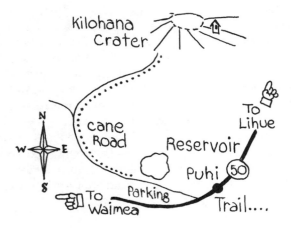

KILOHANA CRATER

(Hiking Area No. 9)

Rating: Hardy family.

Features: Panoramic views, fruits.

Permission: Lihue Plantation Co., Ltd., Mr. Robert Wilson, Controller, Lihue, Kauai 96766.

Hiking Distance & Time: 2.5 miles, 1½ hours, 1000 feet gain.

Driving Instructions: 4 miles, ¼ hour from Lihue. South from Lihue on Route 50, look for large reservoir just off main cane road and park on the shoulder.

Introductory Notes: Kilohana (lit., "lookout point") was once the site of a weekend retreat for pineapple workers. The remains of a house are on the northeast side of the summit.

Legend records that Lahi, a young boy, while hunting birds with his uncle, slew a giant. When warriors came to avenge the death of the giant, the boy

hid and threw them one at a time over the cliff into
the caldera.

On the Trail: The entire trail follows a cane road,
from which you will probably see a variety of cane
operations. You will not see the irrigation systems
that are common on other islands, since most of the
cane in the upland regions depends on rainfall for
water. There is no shade before the summit, so it is a
good idea to wear some kind of headgear.

The sugar-cane cycle includes planting, growth,
irrigation, pest control, tasseling (removing blossoms),
burning off (torching the field to burn away dead
growth, weeds and leaves), and harvesting over a
period of 18-21 months.

Palms at Kapaa

The crater is ringed by strawberry guava (*Psidium cattleianum*). Between August and October this red, walnut-sized fruit flourishes. It may be eaten whole, or after removing the small seeds found inside. The crater is relatively shallow and overgrown with a variety of vegetation; the reward of the trip is the sweeping views of the island, particularly the middle valley region of the east side.

Follow the road to the abandoned house on the northeast side to see some outstanding examples of monkeypod tree (*Samanea saman*). The wood of this tree should be familiar to the visitors for it is widely purchased for gifts in the form of the carved bowls and trays so typical of Hawaii. A symmetrical tree with tiny, delicate pink tufts, the monkey pod will blossom in May and June. The leaves consist of tiny, fernlike leaflets not unlike those of the shower tree. With ample water, it is not uncommon for a monkeypod tree to grow to 80 feet.

In 1882 the Lihue Plantation began a large-scale reforestation program and hired a German forester named Lange to do the job at Kilohana. Consequently, the crater is sometime referred to as the "German Forest." Ironwood (*Casuarina equisetifolia*) was planted to replace dying kukui trees. Although ironwood has little commercial value, it is an excellent windbreak. It resembles a pine because of its long, slender, drooping, dull-green needles.

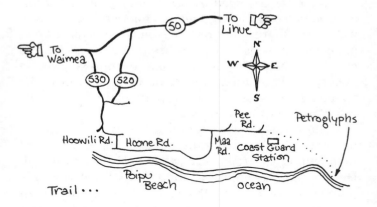

POIPU BEACH PETROGYLPHS

(Hiking Area No. 10)

Rating: Family.

Features: Petroglyphs, burial grounds, swimming, views.

Permission: None.

Hiking Distance & Time: 1 mile, ½ hour.

Driving Instructions: 14 miles, ½ hour from Lihue. South on Route 50, left on Route 520, right on Route 530, quick left on Poipu Beach Road, right on Hoowili Road, left on Hoone Road, left on Maa Road, and right on Pee Road to end by entrance to Coast Guard Station.

Introductory Notes: Poipu (lit., "completely overcast of crashing—as waves") Beach is perhaps the finest swimming, snorkling, surfing and body-surfing area on Kauai. In addition to taking the hike below, you should plan to swim and picnic along Poipu's Beach Road. Be certain to try body surfing at Brennecke's Beach, where the big waves give you an exhilarating ride.

Park on the road just before Loran Station, the Coast Guard Headquarters on Kauai that supervises the lighthouses at Kilauea and Nawiliwili Harbor.

On the Trail: Your hike begins on the most recent volcanic eruption on Kauai, about 40,000 years old. Young in geologic terms anyway, the area is dotted with numerous cinder cones and lava tubes, which some say extend to the ocean. Indeed, as you walk on the hard lava surface, you can hear and feel the rushing water underfoot.

Along the jeep road and in the brush a few plants struggle for survival in an area where the rainfall is light and the soil extremely porous. Ilima (*Sida fallax*) is a small, woody shrub that grows wild. With its small, blunt, bright green leaves and its pale orange, orange or brown flowers, it makes a popular lei. In earlier times only members of the royalty were allowed to wear an ilima lei.

Follow the coast line above Makahuena (lit., "eyes overflowing heat") sand dunes, where in ancient times common people were buried. Children particularly enjoy rolling or sliding down the dunes and hiding in the sandstone caves in ledges along the coast. Find the sandstone ledges at the far end of the beach. Unless the sea or the sand covers them, you will find petroglyphs in the form of human figures, boats, and abstract images that remain a mystery to the experts.

Ilima blossom

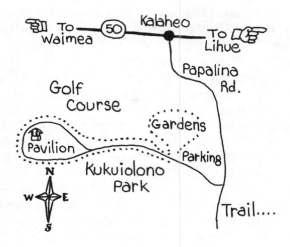

KUKUIOLONO PARK

(Hiking Area No. 11)

Rating: Family.

Features: Japanese Garden, picnic, views.

Permission: None.

Hiking Distance & Time: ½ mile, ½ hour.

Driving Instructions: 12 miles, ½ hour from Lihue. Southwest from Lihue on Route 50, to Kalaheo, left on Papalina Road (1 mile), right at park gate, park by gardens.

Introductory Notes: Walter McBryde, son of one of the earliest European settlers on Kauai, built his home and an elegant park on this hill above the town of Kalaheo (lit., "the proud day") and overlooking Lawai (lit., "seaward") and the beautiful south coast. Today the McBryde estate is a county park and a popular spot to golf, picnic, and stroll through a Japanese garden. Kukuiolono (lit., "light of the god lono") is so named because the hill was used by ancient Hawaiians to signal fishermen at sea and to serve as a beacon.

On the Trail: Park by the gardens and take the short, interesting, pleasant loop around the gardens. The legendary stones of the Hawaiians are particularly notable. The name of each stone indictes its use or significance. For example, there are Lono's Spoon Stone, Awa (fish) Stone, Kauai Iki Stone (shaped like Kauai), Stone Bowl and Stone Salt Pan. Most are three to four feet in circumference. There are also a number of smaller "game stones" which were used in Hawaiian games similar to bowling and the shotput.

The flora in the garden is a mixture of native and introduced plants and trees: crotons, mangoes, kukuis, bananas, papayas, tree ferns, sego pines, and other types of pines, to name a few. The most striking sights are the intricate and delicately beautiful bonsai plants and the flowing "dry stream" of white stone that passes through the garden.

A Mrs. Komaki, a native Hawaiian who married a Japanese man, tends the garden and will enchant you with stories of the past. A friendly, happy, strong, gentle lady, she recalls the day of the "big house" of the McBrydes on the hill above the garden. She also recounts the World War II days, when the house was used to billet U.S. military officers. Like most Hawaiians and locals, she enjoys "talking stories."

As you ascend the hill to the pavilion, you will enjoy the plumeria (*Plumeria acutifolia*) grove along the road. Every color and shade of plumeria seems to be represented. Perhaps the most popular of all lei flowers, the thick, velvety flowers are long-lasting and have a fine fragrance. The white, yellow, pink and cerise plumerias are overwhelming when in full bloom. The milky juice, however, is poisonous and will stain clothing.

The road passes through the golf course, so be on the lookout for flying white balls. You will find water, picnic tables, shelter, and restrooms at the pavilion at the summit: a perfect place to picnic and enjoy the panorama.

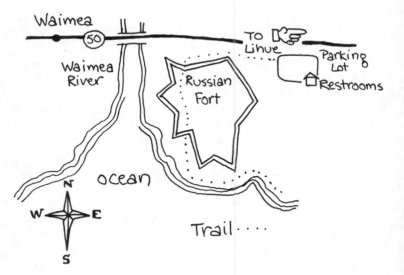

WAIMEA (RUSSIAN FORT)

(Hiking Area No. 12)

Rating: Family.

Features: Historic site, driftwood, dried straw flowers, swimming, views.

Permission: None.

Hiking Distance & Time: ½ mile, ½ hour.

Driving Instructions: 22 miles, ¾ hour from Lihue. Southwest on Route 50 to large parking lot and sign *Fort Elizabeth* on the left (ocean) side of the road just before the Waimea River.

Introductory Notes: In 1817 the Russians secured a foothold on the islands with the construction of a fort that overlooked the Waimea River and the sea. Like the Hawaiians, the Russians used a dry-construction method in which rocks are fitted according to shape, without mortar. The fort was christened Fort Elizabeth. The State of Hawaii plans to reconstruct the fort and to add exhibits. Work on this project was begun in the Fall of 1975. Across the river on the west side is the town of Waimea (lit., "reddish water") and the site of Captain Cook's first landing in Hawaii.

On the Trail: From just east of the bridge, the trail ascends a slight rise on the east side of the river. The thick walls of the fort enable the visitor to walk on top of them for the best view of the fort. A strong imagination is necessary to mentally reconstruct the fort, for the walls and the interior are in disrepair after many years of neglect. A trail snakes through the remains of the fort to the south side, and to the mouth of the river and the beach. One can easily see the commanding position of the fort.

Both inside and outside the fort are a variety and abundance of dried flowers and an assortment of dried "weeds" that make a pretty floral arrangement. Hike from the mouth of the river along the gray-black sand beach to see some interesting driftwood.

Offshore to the southwest lies the tiny island if Niihau, part of Kauai County, which is privately owned by the Robinson family, whose ancestor bought the island for $10,000 in 1864 from the Hawaiian monarchy. Today the island is under a cloud of controversy. Some point to Niihau as the last place where pure Hawaiians live as their ancestors did. Others, applying today's standards, assert that the people live primitively and work for substandard wages and under outrageous conditions. Indeed, some have likened life in Niihau to the feudal system of the Middle Ages. The controversy is heightened by the fact that the outside world is mostly excluded; visits are by invitation only, except for occasional visits by the county tax assessor. Nevertheless, some federal and state educational programs have been accepted and are obviously having an impact on the native population.

Be certain to return to the bridge for impressive views up the river into Waimea Canyon.

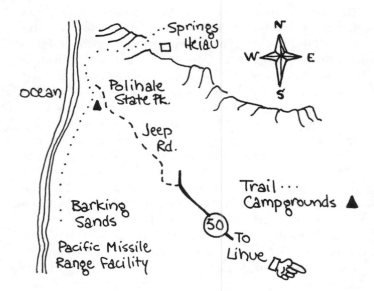

POLIHALE STATE PARK

(Hiking Area No. 13)

Rating: Hardy family.

Features: Camping, swimming, old Hawaiian religious site, springs, views.

Permission: For camping permit write Division of State Parks, State Building, Room 306, 3060 Eiwa St., Lihue, Hawaii, 96766.

Hiking Distance & Time: 3 miles, 1½ hours.

Driving Instructions: 38 miles, 1 hour from Lihue. Southwest on Route 50 to sign *Polihale State Park* just before end of the highway. Left at sign on a dirt/sugar-cane road for 4.7 miles to the end.

Introductory Notes: Polihale (lit., "house bosom") State Park is a fine, relatively secluded place to camp and explore. As at all state parks on Kauai, camping is free and is limited to one week. This was once the site of a famous heiau—a pre-Christian place of worship. The remains, in the form of distinctive rock piles, can be seen along the slopes of the cliffs above the park.

Enjoy the sunset and views of the island of Niihau (see Hiking Area No. 12) and Lehua to its right. The latter is in fact a big rock and the site of the Coast Guard's highest lighthouse, some 7,000 feet tall. In legend Lehua is considered to have been the first landing place of Pele, the fire goddess. The name comes from the story that Pele's sister, Hiiaka, placed a lei of lehua blossoms on it.

On the Trail: From the camping area, it is a hot 3-mile hike south to barking sands beach. Unless you are a sun worshipper, sun protection is well-advised since there is no relief from the hot sun. Wear shorts or hike in a bathing suit for you will want to splash in the surf and take frequent dips in the ocean. Swimming, however, should be approached with caution for the sea can be treacherous, with riptides most of the year.

Polihale State Park

The beach on the way to the sand dunes is somewhat isolated and, therefore, uncrowded. In fact, you probably will not see another person until you reach barking sands. Military personnel and their guests visit the dunes from the U.S. Navy missile facility just south of barking sands.

The barking sand dunes are easy to identify, for some are as high as 60 feet and about ½ mile in area. The name "barking sands" comes from the idea that the sand can be made to give off a dog-like "bark" or "woof" sound. Some visitors have not "heard" a sound and therefore doubt the whole notion, while others insist that they have "heard" a sound, whatever it is. Whatever the fact, try your luck. One of the following methods may be successful for you. 1) Find a dry dune and slide down on foot. While sliding, listen for a deep, sonorous "woofing" sound. 2) Fill a bottle about two-thirds full with sand, shake it, and listen for a sound. 3) Stomp up and down on the side of any dune. After trying all these methods, you are either pleased and fascinated by the "sounds" that you heard or you feel like a damn fool!

Guava

KOKEE STATE PARK/WAIMEA CANYON

(Hiking Area No. 14)

Rating: See individual hikes.

Features: Views of Waimea Canyon and Na Pali Coast, swimming, camping, iliau plant, rain forest, wilderness hiking, wild plums, waterfalls.

Permission: Get camping permit at Division of State Parks, Lihue State Bldg., Room 306, 3060 Eiwa St., Lihue. (Mailing address: Division of State Parks, P.O. Box 1671, Lihue, Hawaii 97666. For cabin reservations write Kokee Lodge, P.O. Box 819, Waimea, Hawaii 96796.

Hiking Distance & Time: See individual hikes.

Driving Instructions: 38 miles, 1½ hours from Lihue to Kokee State Park Headquarters. South on Route 50, right on Route 550 (Waimea Canyon Drive) past Waimea. In Kokee Park, Route 550 becomes State Route 55, although it is not posted as such.

Introductory Notes: Kokee (lit., "to bend or to wind") State Park and Waimea (lit., "reddish water") Canyon are the most popular hiking and camping areas on the island, for obvious reasons. Waimea Canyon has been called the "Grand Canyon of the Pacific." Kokee has numerous hiking trails and untold hunting trails that snake along the pali to otherwise remote and inaccessible places. Everyone is quite taken by the beauty and grandeur of Waimea Canyon. It is about one mile wide, 3600 feet deep, and 10 miles long. While it does not match the magnificence of the Grand Canyon, it has its own unique magic, with its verdant valleys, its lush tropical forest and its rare birds and flora.

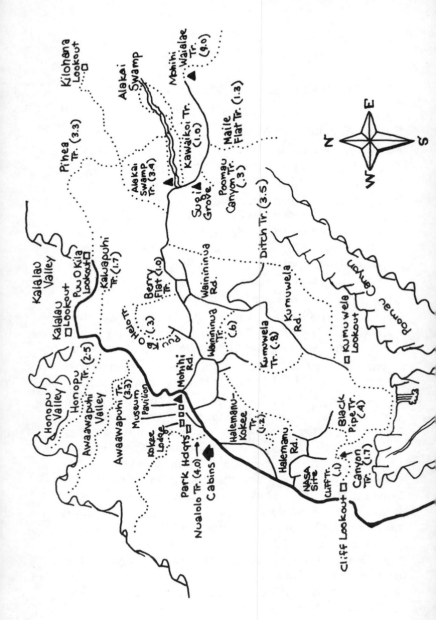

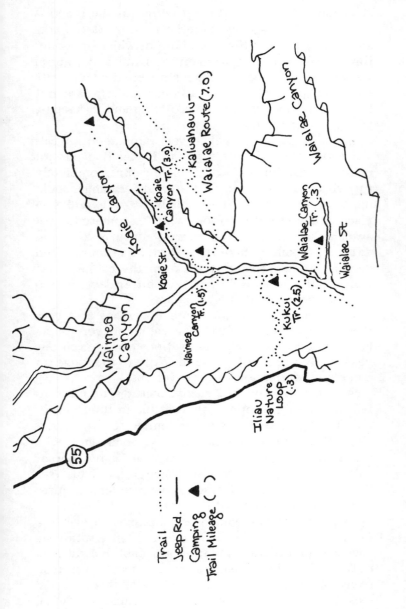

Technically, this northwest corner of the island is under two state agencies, the Division of State Parks and the Division of Forestry, both of which are under the Hawaii State Department of Land and Natural Resources; and Kokee Lodge is operated by a private concessionaire. While the accommodations are not luxurious, they are very comfortable and in keeping with the surroundings.

The state cabins at Kokee, very popular with locals and tourists, require reservations. Kokee Lodge is not really a lodge but rather 12 rustic cabins completely furnished with refrigerator, water heater, range, cooking utensils, shower, linens, blankets, beds and fireplace. All you need is food, which is sometimes not available at Kokee. The nearest store is 20 miles away, in Kekaha. There is, however, a restaurant and cocktail lounge a short walk from the cabins, open from 8:30 a.m. to 5:30 p.m. and on Friday and Saturday evenings for dinner 6-9 p.m.

Each cabin will accomodate 6 persons at a very modest cost of $25 per day. The cabins are very popular with locals, so make reservations early—even one year in advance is not too soon. Write to the lodge for complete information and reservations.

At the north end of a shady, picturesque meadow tent and trailer camping are available in the shade of tall eucalyptus trees. Camping, limited to five days, is free. Water, tables, barbecues, restrooms, and cold-water showers are available. There are a number of wilderness camping areas and shelters available (see the map and the trail descriptions) under the jurisdiction of the Division of Forestry.

In recent years a controversy has existed over the future of the Kokee-Waimea area. Conservationists have sought Federal legislation to establish a national park so that the wilderness can be preserved in relatively pristine condition. Opponents of this proposal seek to retain the present status, because a national park would prohibit hunting, picking plums, and taking plants.

Whatever the future, whether your interest is hiking, hunting or sightseeing, no trip to Kauai is complete without a visit to Kokee and Waimea Canyon. Kokee is also the home of the rare mokihana berry (see the Pihea Trail below), and the even rarer and beautiful *iliau* tree (see the Iliau Nature Loop Trail below) and the delicious Methley plum, which is ready for picking throughout the park in late May and early June. The picking season is short because local people flock to the park and carry off buckets full of this delectable fruit.

On the Trail: Your interests, physical condition, and length of stay at Kokee will help determine which hike you take. On the whole, trails in the general vicinity of park headquarters are relatively short and easy, while trails into Waimea Canyon, to the valley overlooks or into the Alakai Swamp are full-day or overnight trips. Access to most of the trails is from jeep roads that radiate off the main highway—Route 55. You cannot travel these jeep roads in a passenger car even when dry, because many are steep and deeply rutted. The ranger at park headquarters is the best source of information about road conditions.

Following each hike, the mileage from Park Headquarters to the trailhead via the most direct road is noted.

KOKEE—Southwest

Berry Flat Trail, 1 mile, ½ hour (hike rating: family).
Park HQ to trailhead 1.2 miles.

Puu Ka Ohelo Trail, .3 mile, ¼ hour (hike rating: family).
Park HQ to trailhead 0.9 mile.

An easy, pleasant loop trail off Mohihi (a variety of sweet potato) Road combines the Berry Flat and the Puu Ka Ohelo (Ohelo hill) trails.

Both trails pass through scenic forest containing mostly introduced trees that should be easy to identify. Particularly noteworthy is a stand of California redwoods (*Sequoia sempervirens*) that will excite the senses. These wondrous giants tower over the other trees adding a certain majesty to the grove and their droppings provide a luxuriant carpet on which to walk. They are found as you begin the Berry Flat Trail.

In addition, there are stands of Australian eucalyptus, Japanese Sugi pines and the native koa (*Acacia koa*), which grows to a height of more than 50 feet. The koa has a light gray bark that is smooth on young trees and considerably furrowed on mature trees. The leaves are smooth, stiff, and crescent-shaped. Often called Hawaiian mahogany, the wood is red with a wavy grain that makes it popular for use in furniture, woodwork and ukuleles. In older times it had nobler purposes, having been used for war canoes, surfboards and calabashes.

However, the prize to be sought is the popular Methley plum that flourishes in the Kokee area. At the end of the Berry Flat Trail are a number of trees whose fruit ripens at the end of May or the first part of June.

Although no markers are provided, both trails are clear, broad, and easy to follow. You will cross a couple of small streams as you turn onto the Puu Ka Ohelo Trail, where you will find a common vine which is a favorite of wild pigs. The banana passion fruit (*Passiflora mollissima*) is a wild vine that produces a pretty, light-pink blossom and a small, yellow, banana-shaped fruit. The Park Service regards the vine as a pest because it smothers native trees.

There is also a variety of birds along both trails. (All bookstores on the island have small, pocket-sized, inexpensive bird books featuring the most frequently seen birds.) The cardinal (*Richmondena cardinalis*) is a commonly seen bird on the island which was introduced from the mainland. The male, with his all-red body and pointed crest, has been seen along both trails as well as throughout the park.

Black Pipe Trail, .4 mile, ½ hour (hike rating: hardy family).

Park HQ to trailhead 2.5 miles.

This is a short spur trail that connects the Canyon Trail with the middle fork of Halemanu Road. The trail descends into a small overgrown gulch and then climbs to follow the cliff to the Canyon Trail. It is along the pali that the rare and beautiful iliau (*Wilkesia gymnoxiphium*) grows. A relative to the

Iliau plants

rare silversword that grows on Maui, the iliau is endemic to Kauai and found only in the western mountains. It grows 4-12 feet high, it is unbranched, and
the stems end in clumps of long, narrow leaves 6-16
inches long. Once in its life, the plant flowers in a
flourish of hundreds of tiny yellow blossoms.

**Canyon Trail, 1.7 miles, 2 hours (hike rating: stren-
uous).**

Park HQ to trailhead 2.1 miles.

Although the Canyon Trail is steep in parts and
requires some stamina, it offers some of the best
views of Waimea Canyon. The trail begins at the
Halemanu Road and runs south along the east rim of
the canyon. It is somewhat precipitous in places, so
be careful. At the Cliff Lookout, which is 0.1 mile beyond the end of the Halemanu Road, you get not
only a view of the canyon, but also a view of the trail
as it descends and snakes along the cliff.

The Canyon Trail is a popular hike. The trail descends into a gulch and snakes along the cliff to
Kokee Stream and Waipoo (lit., "head water") Falls,
where you can picnic in the shade and swim or splash
in the stream. Go up the stream a short distance for
the best swimming holes.

A common plant on the high, dry ridges is the lantana (*Lantana camara*), which blossoms almost continuously. Its flowers vary in color from yellow to
orange to pink or red; infrequently they are white
with yellow centers. It is a low shrub with a thick,
strong wood.

A small, pretty, yellow-green bird, the anianiau
(*Loxops parva*), is common in the high forests of
Kauai. In truth it is difficult for the less-than-expert
to tell the difference between the anianiau and the
amakihi (*Loxops virents*), which is the same size and
yellow. However, if you get a close look, the amakihi has a dark loral (space between the eye and bill)

mark that joins the eye and the curved dark bill. No matter, however, for they are both pretty birds.

From the falls, the trail makes a steep climb out of the gulch and ascends the pali, from which some of the best vistas of Waimea are had. Once again, be careful for while the trail is broad and easy to follow, steep walls drop to the canyon below. There are numerous places to pause in some shade to enjoy the view through the canyon to the sea on the south side.

After a steep climb, the trail ends at Kumuwela Lookout, from where you can return on the Canyon Trail or connect with the Kumuwela Road or the Ditch Trail.

Cliff Trail, .1 mile, 10 minutes (hike rating: family).
Park HQ to trailhead 2.1 miles.

The Cliff Trail provides a scenic vista of Waimea Canyon and a convenient departure point for the Canyon Trail. It begins after a short walk or drive down Halemanu Road.

Ditch Trail, 3.5 miles, 4 hours (hike rating: strenuous).
Park HQ to trailhead 1.7 miles.

The Ditch Trail is an ambitious hike over some very rough terrain. You can use the trail as part of a loop that also uses the Canyon Trail, or you can enter it from Kumuwela, Wainininua or Mohihi Road. In any event, the trail follows a circuitous route along a cliff and in and out of numerous gulches and small stream canyons.

The trail offers spectacular sights of the interior of Waimea, which is one of the broader and deeper of the canyons. Across the canyon you'll see Kohua Ridge, with its many falls and cascades during rainy periods. Awini ("sharp, bold, forward") Falls is at the southwest tip of the ridge, with Mohihi Falls to the right-rear of the canyon and Moeloa ("to oversleep") Falls to the left-rear of the canyon.

The trail is rich with flora, from the common guava to lehua and a variety of ferns. The variety of tree fern (*Cibotium menziesii*) seen here is the "monkey's trail" fern, with its wiry black hairs on the frond stems. It has the biggest trunk of all Hawaiian tree ferns, a trunk often used for carving akuas (idols) or tikis.

Halemanu-Kokee Trail, 1.2 miles, 1 hour (hike rating: hardy family).

Park HQ to trailhead 0.6 miles.

This is a hike for those who are interested in a short, pleasant, easy walk with the prospect of seeing some native birds and plants. The trail, linking Mohihi and Halemanu roads, is an enjoyable hike in itself and also a route to hiking areas on Kokee's west side. It starts at the old ranger station and ends on Halemanu Road.

Tall trees dominate the area, such as lehua (see Hiking Area No. 6) and the majestic koa (see the Berry Flat Trail above). There are three red birds that you can expect to see along the trail. The cardinal (see the Berry Flat Trail above) has a pronounced crest, which is the most prominent feature distinguishing it from the apapane (*Himatione sanguinea*), a deep-crimson bird with black wings and tail and a slightly curved black bill, and the iiwi (*Vestiaria coccinea*), a vermilion bird with black wings and tail and orange legs. The latter also has a rather pronounced curved salmon bill. Unless you get a good look at these birds, it is difficult to identify them, but they can be enjoyed without being identified. One other bird that is common throughout the forest is the elepaio (*Chasiempis sanwichensis*), an endemic bird that is gray-backed with a rather long, blackish tail and a white rump. It is a somewhat noisy bird, giving forth with what is best described as a sort of "wolf-whistle."

Iliau Nature Loop, .3 mile, ¼ hour (hike rating: family).

Park HQ to trailhead 6.3 miles.

It is 6.3 miles from the campground to the Iliau Nature Loop and the trailhead for the descent into Waimea Canyon. The nature loop is a good place to see some 20 endemic plants, most of which are identified by name plates. The main attraction is the rare and unique iliau plant (see the Black Pipe Trail above). The trail provides a number of vistas for viewing the canyon and Waialae (lit., "mudhen water") Falls on the opposite, west wall of the canyon.

Kaluahaulu-Waialae Trail, 7 miles, full-day hike (hike rating: difficult).

In Waimea Canyon.

This trail is scheduled to become part of an ambitious loop trail covering some 20 miles and extending from the visitor-center area, down Mohihi (Camp 10) Road, across the western portion of the Alakai Swamp, down into Waimea Canyon via Kaluahaulu hill and up the Kukui Trail to the main highway and back to the visitors center.

Presently, the Kaluahaulu-Waialae (lit., Kaluahaulu —"the reddish pit," and Waialae—"mudhen water") Trail is in disrepair and should not be attempted by the novice. The trail was originally constructed by the Civilian Conservation Corps in the 1930's, but is in poor shape as a result of erosion and earthquakes a number of years ago.

The trail from Waimea Stream is easy to follow as it passes through Oneopaewa Valley to the right of larger Koaie Valley. However, the going is very difficult to the point of having to crawl up very steep slide areas that are extremely treacherous. Frankly, the trail should not be attempted alone and not before checking with the Division of Forestry regarding its current condition.

Kaluapuhi Trail, 1.7 miles, 1½ hours (hike rating: hardy family).

Park HQ to trailhead 1.9 miles.

Kaluapuhi (lit., "the eel pit") Trail is a favorite during plum season. If it is a good year (every second year, it seems) for the delicious Methley plum, this trail will take you to some of the best trees. The pickings are generally good due to the fact that the only access to the trees is on foot.

Plum picking is regulated by the state and is limited to 25 pounds of the fruit per person per day. Pickers must check in and out at the checking station, usually located near park headquarters. Many local people bring the whole family and sleep in their cars overnight near the station to get an early start in the morning. A favorite trick of locals is to tout visitors away from the best trees by advising them that they will find the sweetest plums somewhere else.

Access to the trail is a few feet off the main highway where a trail marker identifies the trailhead.

Koaie Canyon Trail, 3 miles, 2 hours (hike rating: difficult).

In Waimea Canyon.

Koaie Canyon is a favorite of hikers and backpackers, for it is an easier trail than Waimea Canyon Trail and it leads to a secluded wilderness shelter. The canyon's name comes from the koaie (*Acacia koaia*) tree, which is endemic to the islands and is much like the koa tree. The wood, however, is harder than koa wood, and was once used to make spears and fancy paddles.

If the water is high in Waimea Stream, you should not hike up-river, since it is necessary to cross the river to the east side to get on the Koaie Canyon Trail. You cross the river just below Poo Kaeha, a prominent hill about 500 feet above the river, pick up Koaie Stream a short distance later, and follow the south side of the stream into Koaie Canyon.

The canyon is a fertile area that was once extensively farmed, as is evidenced by the many terraced areas you'll observe and the rock walls and the remains of house sites. You can usually find ample pools in the stream to swim in or at least to cool off in. During the summer months, the water is quite low, but usually sufficient for some relief from the hot canyon. The Division of Forestry is planning to open a number of wildland campsites in Koaie over the next few years. Presently at trail's end, you'll find Lonomea Camp, an open shelter with table along side the stream near a generous pool for swimming. The Lonomea (*Sapindus cahuensis*) is a native tree with ovate leaves which reaches heights of up to 30 feet. They grow only on Kauai and Oahu.

Don't forget to pack out your garbage.

A Kauai trail

Kukui Trail, 2.5 miles, 2 hours, 2000 feet gain (hike rating: strenuous).

Park HQ to trailhead 6.3 miles.

The Kukui (candlenut lamp) Trail is the short route into Waimea Canyon. A Division of Forestry sign marks the departure point just off the Iliau trail (see the trail description above). Sign in (and out) on the trail register located near the trail's beginning. You may hike and camp in the canyon for three days.

The first part of the trail, dropping over 2000 feet into the canyon, is maintained. Beyond the midpoint, however, the trail is wet and overgrown, and some caution should be exercised. You may have to search out the trail. When in doubt stay out of the heavy growth and bear right.

You'll probably find numerous half-gallon plastic jugs along the trail. They are left by pig and goat hunters as they descend so they will have fresh water on their return. For safety reasons you should stay out of the brush so that you won't be mistaken for a goat or pig by hunters.

The first part of the hike offers some spectacular views of Waimea Canyon and Waialae falls across the canyon on the east wall. The second part of the hike passes through heavy growth until it emerges at Wiliwili (a native tree bearing red seeds). Camp along the boulder-laden banks of Waimea River. It is a delightful spot to camp in shade with ample water from the stream. The water, however, should be boiled or otherwise treated for safety. Many hikers make a base camp at Wiliwili and then hike on the canyon trails and in the side canyons. If you are in good shape, it is possible to make the hike in and out in one day.

Kumuwela Trail, .8 miles, 1 hour, 300 feet gain (hike rating: strenuous).

Park HQ to trailhead 1.0 mile.

At the end of a short spur road off Mohihi Road (see map) turn left into the forest for the beginning of the Kumuwela Trail. The trailhead is not marked. However, the trail dips abruptly into a luxuriant, fern-lined gulch. It is a short hike to Kumuwela Road, where you can connect with the Ditch or the Canyon Trail.

Along this verdant trail there are specimens of lantana, ginger and lilikoi as well as the handsome kukui and koa trees. The trail is well-maintained except for a couple of places that are wet, boggy and overgrown. The last ¼ mile requires a 300-foot elevation gain to the road.

Puu Ka Ohelo Trail, 0.3 mile, 15 minutes.

The trail description is included with the Berry Flat Trail above.

Waialae Canyon Trail, 0.3 mile, ½ hour (hike rating: strenuous).

In Waimea Canyon.

This short, undeveloped trail takes you south along Waimea River from the campground at the terminus of the Kukui Trail. A marker identifies the point where you can ford the river and enter lower Waialae Canyon. The trail follows the north side of Waialae Stream for a short distance to "Poachers Camp," where a shelter, table, and pit toilets are planned for the future.

Waimea Canyon Trail, 1.5 miles, 2 hours (hike rating: strenuous).

In Waimea Canyon.

The Waimea Canyon Trail travels north through the heart of the canyon to the junction of Koaie Stream and Waimea River. Well-maintained, it leads up the river on the west side to a point where a plantation ditchman's house is located. The trail was originally constructed for access to the canyon to construct and maintain a powerhouse up-river.

You reach the trail by hiking down the Kukui Trail to the river, or by hiking seven miles up-river from Waimea town. The latter not only requires permission from a number of private parties but is a hot, exhausting trek. The Waimea Canyon Trail also provides access to the Koaie and Kaluahaulu trails and to the inner recesses of the canyon.

Wainininua Trail, 0.6 mile, ½ hour (hike rating: hardy family).

Park HQ to trailhead 2.2 miles.

Mostly a short, flat, scenic forest walk, the Wainininua Trail with the Kumuwela Trail completes a loop off the Kumuwela Road. There are a variety of native and introduced plants, the most notable being the aromatic ginger (*Zingiber zerumbet*), with its lovely, light-yellow blossoms. Many local girls like to put a fresh ginger blossom in their hair, not only for its beauty but also for its fragrance.

Waimea Canyon

KOKEE—Northwest

Alakai Swamp, 3.4 miles, 3 hours (hike rating: strenuous).

Park HQ to trailhead 3 miles.

Few will disagree that the Alakai (lit., "to lead") Swamp is the most interesting and exciting place on the island. For interest, there is the beautiful mokihana berry—Kauai's flower—and the native rainforests; and for excitement, there is the swamp with its bogs, where a false step puts you knee-deep in mud and water. Be prepared with strong hiking shoes.

The trail begins deceivingly easily off Mohihi (Camp 10) Road, which should be traversed by a four-wheeled vehicle because parts are steep and deeply rutted. (An alternative route is off the Pihea Trail—see below.) A forest-reserve marker identifies the trailhead while the trail follows an old pole line constructed during World War II for Army communications. The trail is well-maintained and easy to follow, as the abandoned poles mark the way.

The first bog is near the one-mile marker. After the Alakai-Pihea Trail junction bogs become more frequent, wetter and deeper until the 2½-mile marker, from where it is all bog until trail's end. Your nose will be your guide to the mokihana (*Pelea anisata*) tree, which emits a strong anise odor. It is a small tree whose small berries are strung and worn in leis. Native to the islands, the mokihana berry is frequently twined with the maile vine to make a popular wedding lei. The maile (*Alyxia olivaeformis*) vine is common along the trail, with its tiny, glossy leaves and tiny, white flowers. Unlike the mokihana tree, the maile vine must be cut or its bark stripped before its musky, woodsy scent of anise is noticed.

After the first two miles of ascending and descending a number of small, fern-laden gulches, the broad, flat expanse of the swamp lies before you. There is little chance of getting off the trail if you follow the pole line, although you may have to circle here and there to avoid the wetter, deeper bogs. At the 2¾-mile marker you must make a left turn, leaving the pole line to follow white and brown pipe markers. With alertness and caution, you'll find your way.

At Kilohana ("lookout point" or "superior") Lookout one has a magnificent view into Wainiha (lit., "unfriendly water") Valley, which extends from the sea to the base of Mt. Waialeale. Beyond Wainiha lies Hanalei (lit., "crescent bay") with its conspicuous wide, deep bay. It's an enchanting place to picnic, rest and reflect.

Alakai Swamp

Awaawapuhi Trail, 3.3 miles, 3 hours (hike rating: strenuous).

Park HQ to trailhead, 1.5 miles.

Of the number of trails that extend to points high above the Na Pali Coast and the extraordinarily beautiful valleys of the north shore, this is the best. You should be in good physical condition before attempting this hike and be prepared with food, first-aid kit, sound hiking boots, and one quart of water per person. The rewards are great, as you pass through tropical forests to view the extremely precipitous and verdant valleys of Awaawapuhi (lit., "ginger valley") and Nualolo.

The trail begins north of Highway 55 at telephone pole No. 1-4/2P/152, about halfway between the Kokee Museum and the Kalalau lookout. There is a forestry trail marker at the trailhead. The trail is well-maintained, and numerous markers show the way.

The trail descends gradually through a moist native forest which becomes drier scrub as it reaches the ridges above the valley. You are most likely to see feral goats in the pali area. With binoculars you can watch goats forage while you picnic on any one of a number of overlooks about 2500 feet above the valley. Additionally, you will probably sight helicopters flying tourists in, out, and over the pali, since the Na Pali Coast is a favorite even of those who are unable or unwilling to make the trip on foot.

At the 3-mile point a trail marker identifies the Nualolo Trail. This trail segment, which is now closed, was once part of a delightful loop hike that led to the main road between the ranger's house and the housekeeping cabins.

The Awaawapuhi Trail continues for 0.3 mile from the junction to a vertical perch above the Na Pali

Coast. This is the best place to lunch and to watch goats. In over a dozen visits to this promontory in recent years, I have seen goats each time. It is a startling and exciting place.

Honopu Trail, 2.5 miles, 2½ hours (hike rating: strenuous).

Park HQ to trailhead 2.0 miles.

Like the Nualolo and the Awaawapuhi trails, this one provides excellent points from which to view the Na Pali Coast. The Honopu (lit., "conch bay") Trail is not as well-maintained as the others. It is dangerous in places where slides make passage along the pali difficult.

The trail begins about ½ mile past the trailhead for the Awaawapuhi Trail north off Highway 55 and snakes along a ridge through dry forested areas and then through scrub forests typical of the area. At numerous points you can picnic and look deep into

Mouth of Waioli River at Hanalei

Honopu Valley, the co-called "Valley of the lost Tribe," where the remains of an ancient Polynesian village have created a mystery as to who were these people and what happened to them.

Kawaikoi Stream Trail, 2.5 (loop) miles, 1½ hours (hike rating: hardy family).

Park HQ to trailhead 3.8 miles.

Access to the Kawaikoi (lit., "the flowing water") Stream Trail is off the Mohihi (Camp 10) Road, which is passable only in a four-wheel-drive vehicle. A 2½-mile loop trail hike was made possible in 1975 when the Forest Service and the Hawaii Chapter of the Sierra Club connected the Kawaikoi Trail with the Pihea Trail.

The route begins opposite a planted forest of Japanese sugi pines and follows the south side of Kawaikoi Stream along an easy, well-defined trail in heavy vegetation. During rainy periods, this is a muddy trail. A short distance past the 0.5-mile point, a trail sign indicates a place to cross the stream to join the Pihea Trail on the north side of the stream. If the rocks are not visible, then the water is too high for a safe crossing. The Kawaikoi Trail itself continues east on the south side of the stream to a point 100 yards past the ¾-mile marker, where a trail sign marks the loop portion of the trail. During the 1-mile loop it is necessary to cross the stream twice.

In recent years, there has been a good deal of grass planting and herbicide work in the area in an effort to control blackberry, which is threatening to take over not only this area but also a number of other areas in the park.

There are many swimming holes in this generous stream and places along the bank to spend some peaceful moments. You may agree with Ralph Daehler, District Forester, who has stated that Kawaikoi is the most beautiful place on Kauai.

Ti plants

Maile Flat Trail, 1.3 miles, 1 hour (hike rating: hardy family).

Park HQ to trailhead 5.5 miles.

Originally constructed by the Civilian Conservation Corps, the Maile Flat Trail is a vigorous hike up Kohua Ridge to Maile Flat, which contains a heavy undergrowth of maile (*Alyxia olivaeformis*). A fragrant vine, maile has glossy leaves, tiny white flowers and a musky, woodsy scent of anise when it is cut or its bark is stripped. Combined with mokihana berries, it is a popular lei for weddings.

From the trailhead, the trail crosses the Mohihi Stream and follows a steep and eroded path to the top of the ridge. It is a popular trail for goat hunters who continue beyond Maile Flat on unmaintained trail.

Mohihi-Waialae Trail, 9 miles, overnight hike (hike rating: difficult).

Park HQ to trailhead 6.2 miles.

The Mohihi-Waialae—and the Waialae Canyon Trail, with which it can form a shuttle hike—are the most difficult trails on Kauai. Do not attempt either without careful preparation or alone. These trails require skill and the aid of a compass, trail-marking tape, a topographic map, and good equipment. The first 4 miles of the Mohihi-Waialae Trail are over a fairly well-defined tread to Koaie Stream. Beyond, the trail is in disrepair as it cuts a circuitious route through the Alakai Swamp to Waialae Stream. Only a skilled hiker with the proper equipment and map can make his way.

The trails begins at the end of the Camp 10 Road, crosses Mohihi Stream, skirts the upper part of the Koaie drainage, continues along a ridgetop to an intersection with the trail to Mt. Waialeale in the Alakai Swamp, and then drops into Waialae Stream Valley to the Waialae Camp area. Camping is permitted both at the Koaie Stream rain gauge and at the Waialae Camp Shelter.

Originally constructed by the Civilian Conservation Corps in the 1930's, the trail segment connecting the Mohihi-Waialae Trail and the Waialae Canyon Trail was largely destroyed by a hurricane in 1959. Presently, the Division of Forestry is reconstructing the trail, and it hopes to complete it soon.

Nualolo Trail, 4.0 miles, 3 hours, 1500 feet loss (hike rating: strenuous).

50 yards west of Park HQ.

This is the third and the easiest of the three trails to the Na Pali Coast. The trail starts between the ranger station and the housekeeping cabins in Kokee. Due to storm damage, the trail no longer connects with the Awaawapuhi Trail. However, the Division of Forestry has plans to construct a connecting trail in the future.

The first part of the trail passes through a native forest of tall trees for a pleasant, cool hike. The trail then descends about 1500 feet to a number of viewpoints overlooking Nualolo Valley. Feral goats, common along the cliffs, can be found foraging in cool, shady places. Carry water and food, for neither is available.

At the 2-mile marker, a spur trail (the old Lolo Bench Mark Trail) goes left, a little-used trail that only goat hunters follow. From the junction the Nualolo Trail goes right and begins to make a more abrupt descent over some badly eroded places where only the sure-footed should pass. Be cautious, for a fall could result in a serious injury. A second junction is reached at the 2½-mile marker. The trail to the right is closed due to storm damage. It used to connect with the Awaawapuhi Trail on the opposite side of the valley. At the 2½-mile junction, bear left for 1½-miles to trail's end and a vista point about 2800 feet above the valley. It is a marvelous place to picnic and to enjoy the solitude.

Pihea Trail, 3.3 miles, 3 hours (hike rating: Strenuous).

Park HQ to trailhead 3.8 miles.

Pihea ("din of voices crying, shouting, wailing, lamentation") Trail is the newest trail—the last 1½ miles were completed in 1975—in the Kokee area. It begins at the end of the highway, 3.6 miles from the campground, at Puu o Kila (lit., "Kila's Hill"), overlooking Kalalau Valley. The first ¾ mile follows the remains of a county road project which was begun in a cloud of controversy and which terminated literally in the mire when money ran out, along with the willingness to continue. A road through the Alakai Swamp and down the mountain to Hanalei would have been a great tourist attraction and an engineering feat, but an ecological disaster.

From the lookout, you can usually see the white-tailed tropic bird (*Phaethon lepturus*) soaring along the cliffs of Kalalau Valley. This bird is white with large black wing patches above and 16-inch white tail streamers. A similar bird that is all white except for red tail streamers is the red-tailed tropic-bird (*Phaethon rubricauda*).

After enjoying the breathtaking views into Kalalau, your trail follows the rim of the valley to Pihea, the last overlook into Kalalau before the Alakai Swamp. The trail makes an abrupt right turn as it enters the swamp and then drops in and out of a number of gulches to the junction with the Alakai Swamp Trail.

The Pihea Trail can be used as part of a loop trip from Kalalau into the Alakai Swamp, with a return to park headquarters via the Alakai Swamp Trail or the Kawaikoi Stream Trail and the Camp 10 Road.

Both the maile vine and the mokihana tree (see the Alakai Swamp Trail for description) are common along the trail and are favorites of both locals and visitors. The mokihana's powerful anise aroma attracts immediate attention.

Also common in this area is the ohia lehua (*Metrosideros polymorpha*), with its tufted red stamens that remind the visitor of the mainland bottlebrush tree. A variety of tree ferns abound along the trail, the hapu'u (*Cibotium chamissoi*) and the amaumau (*Sadleria cyatheoides*) being most common. The latter grows to 10 feet. Its pinnate fronds were once used for huts and the juice from it for a reddish dye.

From the junction with the Alakai Swamp Trail, our trail continues over the newest portion passing through native forests, crossing small streams, and winding through verdant gulches until it joins the Kawaikoi Stream Trail.

Poomau Canyon, .3 mile, 15 minutes (hike rating: hardy family).

Park HQ to trailhead 4.5 miles.

About 0.5 mile past the trailhead for the Kawaikoi Stream Trail on the Camp 10 Road is a marker identifying the Poomau (lit., "constant source") Canyon Trail. This short, easy trail passes through a small stand of Japanese sugi trees, enters a native rainforest, and ends overlooking Poomau Canyon, the largest and northernmost side canyon in Waimea Canyon. Across the canyon on the west rim, the high prominence is Puu Ka Pele (lit., "Pele's hill") and Highway 55. Legend records that Pele, the fire goddess, left Kauai unable to find a suitable home. The caldera was created when Pele brought down her foot for the leap across the channel to Oahu. The caldera has since been filled with small stones by visitors as an offering to the goddess—or so some say. The lookout is an excellent place for pictures of the canyon and for picnicking.

Waialeale Wilderness Trail, 6 miles, 1,500-feet gain, full-day hike (hike rating: difficult).
Off Mohihi-Waialae Wilderness Trail.

Mt. Waialeale is the highest place (5,208 at Kawaikini Peak) on Kauai and the wettest place on the face of the earth, with an annual rainfall between 400 and 600 inches! It also has religious significance for many Hawaiians, with seven of the most sacred heiaus—pre-Christian places of worship—extending from the shore to the summit.

The hike to Mt. Waialeale will always be the most challenging hike on Kauai—or for that matter anywhere on the islands. For the present, however, hikers are discouraged from entering the area pending the results of an environmental impact study and analysis, and, depending upon the results of that study, the construction of a trail.

Over the years a number of daring souls have made the difficult trek off the Mohihi-Waialae Wilderness Trail through seven hard, wet, wind-swept miles of the Alakai Swamp only to find the summit cloud-shrouded and visibility limited to a few feet. Until recently, however, one could avoid the exertion by renting a helicopter ride to the summit and back.

The route—there is no existing trail—to the summit begins about seven miles in on the Mohihi-Waialae Wilderness Trail and leads eastward through the Alakai Swamp. The hike requires sound physical condition, good equipment, a topographic map, a compass, trail-marking tape, and a stout heart. Unless you begin the hike from the Mohihi-Waialae Wilderness Campground, it is not possible to complete a round trip to the summit in one day and since camping is not permitted, it is necessary to complete the hike in one day.

Ralph Daehler, District Forester for Kauai, reported that hiking will be discouraged in the Waialeale portion of the the Alakai Swamp until such time as trails are established and rules and regulations for their use are defined. He noted that Waialaele is an important watershed area and has to be protected.

I recommend the Alakai Swamp Trail for hikers who are interested in exploring the swamp.

Appendix

Division of State Parks
State Building
3060 Eiwa St.
P.O. Box 1671
Lihue, Hawaii 96766

1. camping permits for state parks and for Kalalau Trail

Division of Forestry
State Building, Room 306
3060 Eiwa St.
Lihue, Hawaii 96766

1. hiking information on Kauai

Kokee Lodge
P.O. Box 819
Waimea, Hawaii 96796

1. housekeeping cabin information and reservations

Hawaii Visitor's Bureau
4444 Rice St.
Lihue, Hawaii 96766

1. general travel information

Department of Parks
and Recreation
County of Kauai
4396 Rice St.
Lihue, Hawaii 96766

1. camping permits for county parks (by mail)

County of Kauai
Portable Bldg. #5
4191 Hardy St.
(behind Convention Hall)
Lihue

1. camping permits for county parks (pick up in person)

Index

Alakai Swamp Trail 92-3
Alii shelter 54
amakihi 82
amaumau fern 101
anianiau 82
apapane 84
Australian Kauri tree 48
Awaawapuhi Trail 94-5
Awini Falls 83
banana passion fruit 81
bamboo 37
barking sands beach 74
beach naupaka 32
Berry Flat Trail 80-1
Big Pool 31
Black Pipe Trail 81-2
campgrounds 7
Canyon Trail 82-3
cardinal 81, 84
Civilian Conservation Corps 97, 98
Cliff Lookout 82
Cliff Trail 83
Cook, Captain 1, 71
Daehler, Ralph 103
Davis Falls 31
Dept. of Land & Natural Resources 7, 8, 17, 42, 48
Ditch Trail 83-4
Division of Forestry 7, 8, 42, 45, 78, 87
elepaio 84
eucalyptus tree 47
Fort Elizabeth 70
German Forest 65
ginger 25, 37, 90
goats 29, 30, 94, 95, 99
guava 21, 24, 30, 49, 65
gum trees 43
hala tree 20, 35
Haena campground 8
Halemanu-Kokee Trail 84
Hanakapiai Beach 19, 22
Hanakapiai Falls 22, 25
Hanakapiai Falls Trail 25
Hanakapiai Loop Trail 22, 24-5
Hanakapiai Valley 8
Hanakoa Falls 27

Hanakoa Shack 27
Hanakoa Valley 8, 17, 26-7
Hanalei River 36-8
Hanamaulu campground 8, 10
hapuu fern 101
hau tree 44, 54
Hawaiian language 13
Hawaii Visitors Bureau 4
heiaus 30, 59, 73, 102
Honolulu 1
Honopu Trail 95-6
Honopu Valley 32
Hoolulu Valley 26
Iiwi 84
iliau 81-2, 85
Iliau Nature Loop 85
ilima 67
ironwood 54, 65
Kalalau Trail 4, 17-33
Kalalau Valley 7, 8, 17
Kaluahaulu-Waialae Trail 85
Kaluapuhi Trail 86
Kamapuaa 40
Kawaikoi Stream Trail 96
Keahua Arboretum 42
Keahua Trails 41-51
Kee Beach 19
Kilohana Crater 63-5
Kilohana Lookout 93
koa tree 80, 84
Koaie Canyon Trail 86
koaie tree 86
Kokee Lodge 78
Kokee State Park 7, 8, 10, 77-9
Komaki, Mrs. 69
Koolau 32-3
Kuilau Ridge Trail 50-1
Kukui Trail 88-9
kukui tree 20, 43
Kukuiolona Park 68-9
Kumuwela Trail 89
lantana 29, 82
lauhala 46
Lehua 73, 84
Lihue 4, 8
Lolo Bench Mark Trail 96, 99
Lonomea 87
Lumahai Beach 34-5
Lydgate Park 7, 8, 57-9

Maile Flat Trail 97
maile vine 92, 97
Makahuena dunes 67
Makaleha Mountains 44, 49
Makaweli Ranch 17, 29
mango 24, 39, 59, 62
Mango shelter 27
McBryde, Walter 68, 69
melestoma 46
Menehune 1, 53
milo tree 43
Moalepe Trail 49-50
Moalepe Valley 50
Moeloa Falls 83
Mohihi Falls 83
Mohiki-Waialae Trail 98
mokihana tree 92, 101
Moloaa Beach 39-40
monkeypod tree 46, 55, 65
Mt. Waialeale 43, 102
mountain apples 26, 50
Mu 32
mulberry, paper tree 40

Na Pali Coast 17
Niihau 71
Niumalu campground 10
Nonou Mountain Trails 52-55
Norfolk Island Pine 46
Nualolo Trail 98-9

ohia lehua 45, 101
Okolehau shelter 24
Oopu 45
orchid, Philippine 55

parana pine tree 48
Pele 73, 101
Pihea Trail 99

plum, Methley 79, 80, 86
plumeria 69
Poacher's Camp 90
Pohakuao Valley 29
poi 24
Poipu Beach 66-7
Polihale State Park 7, 8, 10, 72-4
pomelo 37
Poomau Canyon Trail 101-2
prawn, Tahitian 45
Puni 53
Puu Ka Ohelo Trail 80-1, 89
Puu Ka Pele 101
Puu O Kila 99

redwoods 80

Sierra Club 96
Smoke Rock 30

tapa cloth 40
taro 24
Temple of Refuge 58
ti 24
tropicbird 55, 100

Waiahuakua Valley 26
Waialae Canyon Trail 90
Waialae Falls 85
Waialeale Wilderness Trail 102-3
Wailua Falls 60-2
Wailua River 58
Waimea 70-1
Waimea Canyon 1, 77-9
Waimea Canyon Trail 90
Wainiha Valley 93
Wainininua Trail 90-1
Waipoo Falls 82
wiliwili tree 89

See Hawaii as few have –

HAWAIIAN OUTDOOR ADVENTURES

WITH

**HIKING
SWIMMING
SNORKELING
SURFING
FISHING
SHELLING
BEACHCOMBING**

Robert Smith, Author and Outdoorsman

HAWAIIAN OUTDOOR ADVENTURES

17741 Misty Lane
Huntington Beach
California 92649
(714) 840-5888

(WRITE/CALL FOR FREE BROCHURE)